Praise for

THE PROMISE OF A PENCIL

"For anyone with a big dream to transform the world, this book will show you how to get it done."

—Sir Richard Branson

"A compelling and singular story filled with universal truths everyone needs to hear."

—US Senator Cory Booker

"A remarkably inspiring story that shares the essential lessons to creating a life of meaning, passion, and purpose."

—Deepak Chopra, founder of the Chopra Foundation

"Braun's lessons are memorable, accessible, and powerful. This is a must-read, and a must-reread, and a must-keep-in-view-on-bookshelf kind of book."

—Jessica Jackley, cofounder of Kiva

"A vivid, heartfelt account of the power of education and the ability of one person to impact the world."

—Wendy Kopp, founder of Teach For America
and cofounder and CEO of Teach For All

"A perfect step-by-step guide to building the life you've always wanted on your own terms . . . Start reading and don't put the book down until you're finished."

—Gary Vaynerchuk, entrepreneur and *New York Times*
bestselling author of *Jab, Jab, Jab, Right Hook*

"Braun takes you on a mesmerizing round-the-world adventure, while sharing the concrete steps necessary to turn your own ideas into reality. He has his finger on the pulse of what's next and when he speaks you should be listening."

—Keith Ferrazzi, #1 *New York Times* bestselling author
of *Never Eat Alone* and *Who's Got Your Back*

"Adam represents exactly the shift our world needs—one where the brightest minds of our generation focus on addressing the most important problems of our time. The more people read his story, the more this shift will accelerate."

—Ben Rattray, founder and CEO of Change.org

"Adam nails a truth we live by. The biggest difference between the person who lives their dream and the person who continues to dream is their decision to take the first step—even if the second step is unknown. Honest and entertaining. A great read."

—Ben Nemtin, #1 *New York Times* bestselling author and cocreator of *The Buried Life*

"Adam's story is iconic and riveting. *The Promise of a Pencil* will inspire the next generation of social entrepreneurs and persuade readers to lead lives of purpose."

—Charles Best, founder and CEO of DonorsChoose.org

"Grab a hot chocolate and read this book. No better feeling in the world than being inspired by a blazing story in one hand and a hot cocoa in the other."

—Nancy Lublin, CEO of DoSomething.org

"Adam Braun has built a wonderful organization that provides education and a solid start to children around the world. His journey captured here should inspire others to similarly follow their hearts and passions in making the world a better place."

—Lauren Bush, founder of FEED

"*The Promise of a Pencil* is a great read for anyone who has ever felt a restless idea brewing inside but lacked the inspiration or know-how to take the next step."

—Scott Harrison, founder and CEO of charity: water

"Adam Braun is a leader among an emerging generation of change makers who are proving that every person can be a force for positive change."

—Ann Veneman, former executive director of UNICEF

"With relentless optimism and the idealism of a seasoned traveler, Adam Braun tells an incredibly personal story about his journey from student to philanthropist. What's so extraordinary about Braun's story is how he built a simple gesture of kindness—one pencil for one child—into a movement that has inspired and influenced a new generation of philanthropists and entrepreneurs. And he's just getting started."

—Jared Cohen, bestselling author and director of Google Ideas

"[An] exuberant testimony to the power of idealism . . . Braun's story forcefully presents the advantages of silencing the head and listening to the heart."

—*Publishers Weekly* (starred review and Book of the Week)

THE
PROMISE
OF A PENCIL

How an Ordinary Person
Can Create Extraordinary Change

ADAM BRAUN

with Carlye Adler

SCRIBNER
NEW YORK   LONDON   TORONTO   SYDNEY   NEW DELHI

Scribner
A Division of Simon & Schuster, Inc.
1230 Avenue of the Americas
New York, NY 10020

Copyright © 2014 by GoodPenny Ventures LLC

First Scribner trade paperback edition February 2015

SCRIBNER and design are registered trademarks of The Gale Group, Inc., used under license by Simon & Schuster, Inc., the publisher of this work.

For information about special discounts for bulk purchases, please contact Simon & Schuster Special Sales at 1-866-506-1949 or business@simonandschuster.com.

The Simon & Schuster Speakers Bureau can bring authors to your live event. For more information or to book an event contact the Simon & Schuster Speakers Bureau at 1-866-248-3049 or visit our website at www.simonspeakers.com.

Interior design by Jill Putorti
Cover photograph © Nick Onken

Manufactured in the United States of America

10   9

Library of Congress Control Number: 2014000425

ISBN 978-1-4767-3062-2
ISBN 978-1-4767-3063-9 (pbk)
ISBN 978-1-4767-3064-6 (ebook)

To my two greatest heroes,
my mother and father

Don't ask yourself what the world needs.
Ask yourself what makes you come alive and then go do that.
Because what the world needs is people who have come alive.

—HOWARD THURMAN

CONTENTS

THE
PROMISE
OF A PENCIL

INTRODUCTION

On a sunny autumn afternoon just before my twenty-fifth birthday, I walked into a large bank in my hometown. At the time, I had everything I thought would make me happy—the job, the apartment, the life. My closet was full of impressive corporate clothing, and my business card carried the name of a prestigious company that garnered respect in every room I entered. I looked like a guy on the right path who was most likely walking into the bank to deposit his monthly paycheck.

But deep down inside, I was no longer enamored with the life I'd created. The only purpose I was serving was self-interest. While I rarely showed it to outsiders, my happiness waned day after day. A restless voice kept me up at night, telling me that until I found meaning, the money wouldn't matter. It told me that I'd find far more fulfillment if I measured my life in purpose, not profits. And that I didn't have to keep waiting, that now was the perfect moment to start chasing my biggest dreams.

It's strange how you can sometimes feel a yearning that seems bigger than your actual body. That's how I felt that day. I wanted to be a part of something that extended far beyond my two hands and the possessions they could hold. No matter how scared I was of getting off my safe path, I needed to see what would happen if I finally stepped into the uncharted territory where unbridled ambition and opportunity reside.

The scariest part was that I wasn't some successful businessman who'd built and sold companies. I didn't have a lengthy career to prove I would succeed. Nor did I have millions of dollars in financial backing. I was just a regular guy with $25 who wanted to prove that regardless of age, status, or location, every person has the capacity to change the world. So I used that small amount to open a new account in hopes of one day building a school. Everything that came after was a result of that first step. That leap of faith rippled outward, spanning cultures and continents.

Since then I've immersed myself in the field of global education. I believe that where you start in life should not dictate where you finish. And that no tool can more profoundly unlock a person's ability to change his or her place in life than access to quality education. The good news is that we have the ability to provide quality education to every child on earth right now. We are not looking for a miracle vaccine or drilling for a hidden resource that may not exist. We have all the tools necessary at this very moment. Yet we still have 57 million children out of school, and millions more who sit in classrooms each day but remain illiterate.

Education is a complex issue, which requires a complex set of solutions. There is no silver-bullet answer to educating the children of the world, but the global education crisis remains the single most solvable and important human rights issue of our time. The knowledge that it *can* be solved gives me hope and purpose. But no individual can solve the world's problems alone. A collective effort is required, and we each have a unique role to play.

This is the story about what happens when you acknowledge that there's more for you to become, and that you don't have to have enormous resources to make a difference in the world. It's a story about what can unfold when inspiration strikes and you realize that the rewards of living a purposeful life are rich and lasting. It's the story of my life (although I have changed the names of several people at their request), but it's a story that can belong to anyone.

Each of the thirty chapters in this book is titled with a mantra. These mantras have served as my guideposts as I've faced decisions both large and small. They have become my essential truths. I've written them with the hope that they will be carried forward, shared with others, and adopted in ways that help you on your own journey as well. Each story stands on its own, but taken together they create a roadmap that I hope will enable you to turn your own dreams into reality.

If one of these stories ignites something within you, listen to that restless feeling that your head may tell you to ignore but your heart will tell you to pursue. The biggest difference between the person who lives his or her dreams and the person who aspires is the decision to convert that first spark of motivation into immediate action. Take the first small step, then chase the footprints you aspire to leave behind. Every person has a revolution beating within his or her chest. I hope that this book helps you find yours.

WHY BE NORMAL

Although we never officially assigned the seats around our dinner table, we always knew our places on Friday nights. My dad sat at the head, with my brother and me to his right, my sister and my mom to his left. We usually had a few friends and extended family who joined too. Every week the cast of characters changed slightly, but the fervor of debate always remained the same. And more often than not, the heat came directly from the head of the table.

My father was known in my hometown as the intimidating dad. He coached and played nearly every sport with unmatched intensity: basketball, baseball, football—he dominated them all. He felt that kids in our town were coddled, and he would make sure they knew it: "Stop being such lily-white-bread pussies!" he'd scream at the twelve-year-olds on my basketball team. When he gave us praise, it was carefully delivered, and it meant something. He wanted us to earn it—through mental toughness and a tenacious work ethic. Because of this, most kids both loved and feared him. He was an old-school disciplinarian and didn't mind letting people know it.

As my siblings and I entered adolescence, he developed code words for us, which he would use to warn us that we were about to go over a line we did not want to cross. He'd use these code words in conversation, at the dinner table, or in public to say, "This is your last warning, do not push my buttons anymore." My older brother, Scott, is a typical firstborn son; he loved to challenge my dad's authority. His code word was Cream. Mine was Ice, and my younger sister, Liza, was Sundae. If we were all misbehaving, upsetting my mother and about to catch a spanking, my dad just had to yell "Ice Cream Sundae!" and we would stop right away. But as I look back on it, being the guy furiously screaming "Ice Cream Sundae!" probably didn't help to rid my father of his reputation among my friends of being "the scary dad."

Even back then, we knew his crazy temper and strict discipline were just forms of tough love. He wanted to get the best from each of us—and he got it. As a coach, no one pushed me harder. He had me play three games on the final day of the 14-Year-Old State Championships with a raging fever because he knew how badly I wanted to win the tournament. He'd set up cones in the basement so that after dinner I could do dribbling drills in the dark. But the result was worth it. And when I consider what motivated my siblings and me most, it all boiled down to one phrase that my dad used constantly that gave us the permission and the directive to stand out. He loved to remind us, "Brauns are different."

My siblings and I knew that some of the parents in town rewarded their kids for good grades. This could mean up to $100 for an A,

$75 for a B, $50 for a C, and so forth. When I asked my parents for some form of compensation for my academic performance, my request was shot down immediately.

"Paul Mazza just got one hundred and fifty dollars for good grades. Can I get something?" I'd ask.

"Brauns are different. You have our gratitude," they'd say.

During Hanukkah, rather than receiving eight nights of gifts, we received gifts on only four nights, and the alternate four nights we selected a charity that my parents donated to in our names. When we'd ask why half of our Hanukkah gifts were charitable donations instead of presents, my parents would simply respond, "Because Brauns are different."

Most of our friends had high-tech toys and video games, but my siblings and I were told to go read books or play outside. Our pleas and arguments were always met with the same response: "Brauns are different." My dad didn't think we were superior, he wanted us to hold ourselves to a higher standard.

This phrase was not only used to justify my mom and dad's different approach to parenting, but to celebrate us when we displayed courage by taking the path less traveled. If we stood up for a classmate who was being bullied, they would applaud us by saying, "You know why you did that? Because Brauns are different." Children want nothing more than their parents' approval, and pretty soon we developed an inherent drive to live into the ideals they had defined for us.

Every night before we went out to parties in middle and high school, my dad would say, "Remember Dad's Rules." Dad's Rules meant "Don't do anything that you wouldn't do if Dad were watching. Choose your actions as if Dad were next to you the whole time."

These expectations of excellence became the tent poles that formed our values, and our values then guided the choices we made. They served as a constant reminder that to achieve exceptional things, you must hold yourself to exceptional standards, regardless of what others may think. My dad even went so far as to order license plates that read YBNML, which my scared middle school friends always assumed meant "why be an animal." The real meaning was much more apt: "why be normal."

My dad's intensity and belief in the power of nonconformity no doubt were born from his parents' experiences. When she was fourteen, my grandmother Eva (known to us as Ma) and twenty-seven family members including her mother and twelve-year-old sister were forced from their home in Hungary and placed in a ghetto with the other Jews from their town. From there, they were transported in cattle cars to the most feared of concentration camps, Auschwitz. Upon their arrival, people were lined up before camp doctors and ordered to go left or right. Ma's entire family was ordered to go left, but because she was of working age, the doctor insisted that she walk to the right. As a scared young girl, she cried and refused to leave her mother and sister's side. The Nazi guards beat her until she was unconscious. When she woke up, she pleaded with the other camp prisoners to tell her where she could find her family. With grim faces, they pointed to the smokestacks. Her entire family were sent to the gas chambers, killed, and cremated the day of their arrival in Auschwitz.

After six months in the camp, surviving brutal conditions and watching countless others die next to her each day, Ma was transported to a new concentration camp. In her words, "Bergen-Belsen camp was even worse than Auschwitz. You were only there to die." But Ma believed that her father would be waiting for her when the war was over, and the belief that she needed to survive to make sure he had at least one other family member kept her spirit strong enough to go on each day. That sense of purpose enabled her to survive through conditions in which many others perished.

After she spent eight months in Bergen-Belsen, the war ended and British GIs liberated her from the camp. She was so weak that she could not feed herself, which ultimately saved her life because others fed her slowly enough to allow her stomach to readjust to solid foods. She had nearly starved to death, and she would not allow that fate for her grandchildren. Later she became almost obsessed with watching us eat. She often spent days preparing chicken-noodle soup, brisket, ice-cream sandwiches, and chocolates for us to fill our bellies with on Friday nights. As soon as one plate was finished, another whopping portion appeared. "There's dessert too, my angels," she would say, nodding with approval.

Once recovered, Ma took that long-awaited ride back to Hungary to find her father. While others reunited with loved ones in tears of joy, she found herself alone at the train station in Budapest. Her father never came. He had been killed at a work camp in Russia. No one came. Devastated, she phoned the only other relative she thought might be alive, her uncle, and he offered to take her in.

A few years later, Ma's uncle offered to introduce her to a friend of his, Joseph, who was also a Holocaust survivor. He had lived through a year at the Dachau concentration camp, where both of his younger brothers and his father were killed. Through his persuasion, persistence, and a shared understanding of loss, they created a profound bond. Joseph Braun soon asked Eva to marry him, and after they were married, she gave birth to a girl and a boy. The boy, Ervin Braun, is my father. When the Hungarian Revolution broke out in 1956, they planned an escape across international borders to the safety of the United States. My grandfather (whom we called Apu) tested the route first, fleeing alone across the Hungarian border at night and then returning to gather his mother, sisters, wife, and children.

After they stowed away in a packed boat of immigrants, traveling thirteen days across the Atlantic Ocean to arrive in New York City, my father and his family spent their first nights on American soil in a Jewish refugee camp. With the assistance of a relief organization, they found a one-bedroom apartment in Crown Heights, Brooklyn. My grandfather worked as a dental technician making fake teeth, and my grandmother worked in a sweatshop. For ten years she worked for just $1 per day, knitting garments in horrific conditions so that her children and future grandchildren could live a better life.

My dad learned to speak English without an accent by diligently studying the way Americans pronounced words on television shows such as *The Lone Ranger* and *The Little Rascals*. He was a star student, skipping eighth grade and attending Bronx High School of Science. His parents were so fearful of their only son's getting hurt, they wouldn't sign the permission slips to let him play on any local sports teams. Instead, he waited for his parents to go to work and then snuck out to play basketball and football on the city playgrounds.

For as long as my dad could remember, his parents wanted him to become a successful dentist. After completing college in three years, he chose to attend the University of Pennsylvania for dental school, where he'd meet a woman who would change the trajectory of his life: my mother, Susan, a country girl from a humble town in the Catskills. Her father, Sam, had escaped Poland to avoid persecution just before the Holocaust began, but passed away when my mom was eleven years old. Her mother, Dorothy, raised her with an emphasis on morality and civic responsibility. My mother's favorite word is *integrity*, as it's the quality she was raised to value most.

During the first weekend of my mother's freshman year at UPenn, my dad went to a college party where he met her older sister, Lynn. The next day he thought he saw Lynn walking down some stairs and called her out by name. But it wasn't Lynn; it was my mother, Susan. She blew him off completely, which of course piqued his interest. He began to pursue her, and after their first date he told his friends, "I'm going to marry that girl." He even went so far as to write it on a piece of paper and place the message in an empty bottle on his mantel, where it stayed until he revealed it to her at their wedding.

Once my parents were ready to start their own practices as a dentist and an orthodontist, they put together a list of what they wanted most and rated each of the surrounding communities accordingly. Education was the most important criterion, and Greenwich, Connecticut, had the best public schools. The town also had a culture of volunteerism that my mother craved and a growing diversity that my father wanted his children exposed to. They got a loan to buy a property in Cos Cob, the historically blue-collar, Italian part of town that was inhabited by the service workers who built the town's mansions in the 1950s. We moved there when I was a young boy, and that's where my earliest memories were formed.

By the time I reached high school, I played basketball year-round. One weekend, two tall African boys joined my team for a summer tournament in Albany. They towered over the others—Sam was six feet six inches and Cornelio six feet nine inches—but I immediately sensed their warmth and kindness. They were childhood friends from Mozambique who found themselves bound together on a journey to the States in search of education.

During the weekend tournament, we became fast friends. On the drive home from Albany, Sam and Cornelio asked if they could stay with my family for the five days until the following weekend's tournament. We readily agreed, considering we were always hosting teammates, friends, and family. But when the second tournament ended, they asked my dad, "Can we stay next week too?"

Sam and Cornelio were supposed to be living in Philadelphia, where they had been for the past eight months. But they were vehement about not going back—not even to pick up their stuff. When we asked why, they told us how they had been lured to America under the false promise of a fantastic education. Their families put $1,000 toward their flights, yet upon arrival in the United States, they were ushered into a makeshift apartment in the slums of South Philadelphia. The "school" they were supposed to be attending was a single classroom in the back of a run-down church. A teacher came in at the start of the day, passed out textbooks to the twenty-five boys there, and left. The school was simply a front for a scam-artist-turned-basketball-coach to recruit players. He lured them to the States and then sent them to colleges that were affiliated with shoe companies, based on whichever shoe company paid him more. If one of these players made it to the NBA, the sponsoring shoe company would have the inside track, but none of these kids received a real secondary education along the way.

In their second week staying at our house, my brother was home from college and drove Sam and Cornelio to Greenwich High School, the public school I now attended. Their eyes lit up. They had traveled thousands of miles to attend a great school. They saw the chance to realize their American dream and asked us to take them in as their legal guardians within the United States so they could attend our local public high school.

Given my dad's background as an immigrant, the boys' story resonated with him deeply. We had hosted hundreds of kids overnight at our house, but something about Sam and Cornelio was unique. They were both so genuine and humble, and they embodied the kind of integrity my family valued so much. My mother and my sister were completely won over by them, and Scott, who was scheduled to return to Emory in Atlanta that fall, was especially hyped about the idea.

One night, my parents asked to speak with me privately. They told me about the boys' request for us to take them into our family and informed me that the final decision was up to me. "It's going to fall on you to chaperone them, tutor them, and assimilate them into school. You're also applying to colleges this fall, so we know you're under a lot of stress, and this decision is going to impact you the most right now. The rest of us are willing to take them in, but it's your choice."

When you come from a lineage of Holocaust survivors, you grow up with an understanding that everything was once taken away from your family. The only things that enabled them to survive and then radically change their lot in life were the strength of their willpower, the help of others, and a commitment to education. Sam and Cornelio had demonstrated willpower and a hunger for education in abundance. They just needed a little bit of help. People with nothing to gain had once stepped in to help my family, and now I had the opportunity to pay it forward.

Later that night I told my parents that I wanted us to take in the boys as well. My parents soon became Sam and Cornelio's legal guardians within the United States. They enrolled in Greenwich High School with my sister and me—and became our two new brothers.

Our Shabbat dinners on Friday nights looked a little different with two huge African kids towering over the table, but the real transformation that took place within our family was much more profound. While my parents gave these boys an incredible opportunity to change the trajectory of their lives, what they gave us was much more. They changed us. They certainly changed me.

For the first time, I began to fully understand that there was a vast world outside of the towns and neighborhoods I had come to know. I started to think about what it would be like if our roles had been reversed and I had grown up in Mozambique rather than them. I wondered if I would have had their same courage to leave home and venture into unknown lands.

The more I learned about the challenges they had overcome, the more I grasped the qualities necessary to change one's path. Sam and Cornelio were the only ones among their friends and family to depart from the life that was expected of them. They did not follow the norms of their peers. They chose to be different. And in doing so, they proved that through struggle, sacrifice, and service, staggering personal transformation is possible.

Mantra 2

GET OUT OF YOUR
COMFORT ZONE

Wherever you grow up, your surroundings are your measuring stick. Although my parents were a dentist and an orthodontist, many of my friends' parents were investment bankers, hedge-fund managers, and CEOs. We knew as kids that among the parents in the crowd at our local football games, a handful of multimillionaires usually could be counted. Once I fully grasped that some of my friends' parents made tremendous amounts of money while others made very little, my love of competition and numbers soon morphed into a new obsession—Wall Street. By the time I was in middle school I was fixated on working in finance and becoming a billionaire.

In middle school I opened an E*TRADE account to buy and sell shares of Gap and Nike. By the time I was sixteen I started working at a hedge fund during my summer break, trying to learn everything I could about the financial markets. When I was nineteen, I worked at a fund of funds and went to New York City, not to see a show or buy knockoff watches on St. Mark's Place, but to visit the New York Stock Exchange and spend time on the trading floor.

During those same years, I developed an entrepreneurial instinct and started a revolving door of small businesses. My first paid job at age twelve was manual labor, cleaning people's yards and moving their furniture for $6 per hour. But I soon realized that with the rise of eBay, I could burn and sell rare CDs of live concerts for $40 each. I immediately quit carrying lawn chairs into people's basements and was soon making thousands of dollars a year shipping CDs around the country. My parents made it clear to us that we weren't going to have any trust funds waiting for us one day. If we wanted something, we would have to work for it and pay for it ourselves. So I was never comfortable working just one normal job. If there was a small business to be started, I was constantly evaluating how to make it happen.

My desire to become an investment banker led me to study economics at Brown. I had been recruited to several schools to play basketball, but chose Brown because I could fulfill my dream of playing a Division I sport while also pursuing my academic interests. I immediately began taking courses in sociology, management, and entrepreneurship, including Engineering 90 (affectionately known as Engine 90) with Professor Barrett Hazeltine, the same class that gave rise to the juice company Nantucket Nectars. Each student was required to write a business plan for a potential company, and for the first time I started to learn the formal side of the management world.

My path toward a lucrative job in finance was progressing well; I was a student-athlete on my way toward the life I'd always dreamed of, filled with cars, boats, and a luxurious house. I was working multiple jobs on campus, the basketball team was on its way to one of the best seasons in school history, and I seemed to have everything on track. My family and friends thought my grand plan was aligning perfectly, but internally I was beginning to ask fewer questions about money and more questions about meaning.

As my sophomore year was coming to a close, I went to a nearby dorm to watch a movie called *Baraka* with my friend Luke. He'd told me, "This film is the most beautiful thing I've ever seen and will change the way you look at the world."

Baraka means "blessing" in many languages. The movie had no formal actors, no plot, and at first I had no idea what was going on, but I knew it was spectacular. The film was a series of scenes shot all around the world that showed stunning geographic wonders juxtaposed with ceremonies and customs of indigenous cultures. The film spanned twenty-four countries—the towering ruins in Indonesia, the killing fields in Cambodia, the chaos and color of India.

One scene in particular captivated me. It began with a mass of people wading in a river of dirty water, praying, giving oblations. A man was carrying something ornate on his shoulders with smoke rising from it. A woman cupped the river water in her trembling hands, clearly in reverence to its holiness. Fires burned all around the riverbanks. In the last seconds of the scene something charred appeared. It took me moments to recognize it, but then it hit me. At one end was a face; at the other end was a foot. It was a human being burned.

I felt as if I had been kicked in the stomach. I had no idea where this scene was filmed or why it was happening, but I knew it was real, and it was spiritually significant. All I could think was, *If everything I'm seeing in this film is actually happening somewhere on the*

planet, right now, at this very moment while I'm sitting in this dorm
room, then I need to go to these places and see this with my own eyes. How
could I grow up in Connecticut, attend college in Rhode Island,
and then move to New York City without seeing other cultures
besides my own?

I bought the movie and invited others over for viewing parties. Every time I watched it I discovered something new and felt
a deepening desire to explore the vast expanses beyond my insular
surroundings.

I searched the Web for the location of the holy-river scene and
discovered it was in Varanasi, the spiritual capital of India. The
city sits on the left bank of the Ganges River, the holiest water in
India. The river is considered a god itself, and according to Hindu
legend the area was founded by the god Shiva. Younger Hindus
wash away their sins in the religious waters while the elderly and
the sick hope to die in Varanasi as a way to achieve nirvana. I knew
I needed to go there.

I left the basketball team knowing I needed some time to
myself, and started to explore my spirituality and faith. I wanted to
understand why I should believe in my religion over all the others,
so I began to meet weekly with a rabbi to study the Torah. I also
began intensely researching different faiths and spiritual beliefs,
spending time in the library, where every month I would focus
on reading the texts of a different religion: Taoism, Hinduism,
Christianity, Buddhism, Islam, and so on. Rather than assuming
everything I had been taught was true, I reversed my approach to
challenge all of my existing assumptions and only decided to adopt
that which I could believe on my own.

While high school encouraged conformity, college taught me
it was okay—even desirable—to question what I thought I knew. It
was an awakening. For the first time, I began to explore and cele-

brate my quirks and unique interests. I read books like *On the Road*, *1984*, and *Man's Search for Meaning*, each of which encouraged individuality and discovery of purpose. The music I listened to changed from modern pop acts to artists whose lyrics were just as powerful as their instrumentation, like Bob Dylan, Richie Havens, and Van Morrison. Their lyrics became my scripture. I began to see that success in life isn't about conforming to the expectations of others, but about achieving personal fulfillment. Your twenties are the time to both accept and fight your way into the person you're destined to become. Through the books I read, the music I obsessed over, and the late-night conversations I shared with friends and strangers, I began to craft my identity separate from the whims and expectations of others.

Going through so much personal change led me to explore the possibility of spending time abroad the next year. I looked at various locations in India as well as South Africa and Southeast Asia. Eventually my dad made an alternative suggestion: "You should look into Semester at Sea [SAS]. One of my patients just got back and raved about it."

Although at first I was skeptical, the more I looked into the program, the more impressed I was by the opportunity to travel to ten different countries and then backpack independently for the first time.

I wanted to be challenged. As strange as it sounds, I wanted to know what it's like to be truly uncomfortable. So many of the people I admired—the musicians, the artists, the writers—created their greatest works not during a period of happiness and contentment, but during a period of struggle. The majority of the songs I loved were anthems inspired by war, unrequited love, or civil revolt.

Many of us spend our entire lives in the same bubble—we surround ourselves with people who share our opinions, speak the way we speak, and look the way we look. We fear leaving those familiar surroundings, which is natural, but through exploration of the unfamiliar we stop focusing on the labels that define *what* we are and discover *who* we are.

The next month, I applied to SAS and was accepted. I didn't tell anyone besides my parents because I knew that some of my high school and college friends would want to join. I loved and respected those friends, but I wanted to be alone on this journey. I wanted to see how I would react without the familiarity of my past dictating the steps toward my future.

In the days leading up to my departure I nervously scribbled in my journal, "The experience of a lifetime begins. . . . I'm going to leave everything behind, my biases, my expectations, my comforts, my friends, and my family. I don't know exactly how these 100 days will affect me, but I know I'll be a changed man."

True self-discovery begins where your comfort zone ends, and mine was about to end far more quickly than I'd anticipated.

KNOW THAT
YOU HAVE A PURPOSE

Sunrise seeped into my cabin through a small porthole, where just hours earlier I watched thirty-five-foot swells rise like mountains in the distance. I'd woken up with my bed tossed diagonally across a room that I no longer recognized. My tiny dresser, with the drawers I had taped shut to keep from hearing them open and slam closed, open and slam, was flipped on its side. Clothes and textbooks carpeted the floor. My cherished Canon SD300, cracked, lay on the ground. I looked over at my roommate, Jaret, who was usually so upbeat and always writing furiously in his journal. He was pale and locked with fear. I couldn't figure out what was happening, but I knew it couldn't be good.

At least my headache was gone.

I'd forgotten to pack my Excedrin PM, so the night before when a horrific migraine took hold of me, I swallowed an Ambien to knock me out. I wasn't a stranger to sleep aids; I'd been taking them to battle bouts of insomnia since high school. Ambien didn't lull me to sleep; it pinned me in a deep slumber and held me there against all odds.

"What the hell happened in here?" I asked Jaret. I attempted to stand, and the room swayed to its side. We braced ourselves against our beds.

"The past few hours have been insane," he said with a panicked look. I didn't remember any of it, but he said he was awoken at 3:00 a.m. by heavy items sliding across our cabin—dressers, beds, tables—so he went out into the hall, where he thought he'd be safest. Most of the other people on our hall did the same. After an hour, Jaret returned to the room to say a few prayers, write down some thoughts, and check on me. Apparently while the world was crashing down around us, my Ambien was functioning properly.

Thirteen days earlier, I'd boarded the MV *Explorer* cruise ship in Vancouver, British Columbia, eager to start Semester at Sea. On the hundred-day trip we would circle the globe, opening our senses to cultures on four continents. It would be the trip of a lifetime.

But as soon as we left the port, bound for South Korea, we met rough seas. Low-pressure air currents swept across the icy northern rim of the Pacific, churning the waters around us. During winter the older Semester at Sea ships usually sailed the more expensive, but safer, east-to-west route, but our brand-new vessel would attempt a North Pacific crossing.

As the ship's swaying increased with each passing day, students began popping Dramamine like Skittles to quell their queasy stomachs. Nonetheless, spirits remained high. We stumbled from class to class and made bad jokes about "finding our sea legs." When lunch plates slid off the tables during meals, we laughed with giddy excitement. This was an adventure. We were 650 college students aboard a twenty-four-hundred-ton vessel, powered by mighty twin engines. We were invincible.

We didn't have TV and the Internet was expensive and slow, so we created nightly diversions to entertain ourselves. We read Lonely Planet guidebooks, played board games from our childhood like Monopoly and Scrabble, and spent hours debating guitarists and G-d.

Day after day the storms grew worse, but we had complete confidence in the ship's leader, Captain Buzz, a gray-haired seafarer with a Southern drawl. When Captain Buzz gave directives, we listened. And when he said we'd be fine powering through the rising storms, we believed him.

Every day, Captain Buzz gave us a weather update and a list of the ship's coordinates. Google Maps wasn't a part of our daily life yet, so students anxiously wrote down the longitude and latitude of our current position, then later used them to figure out the ship's location on an actual map. An administrator known as the dean of student life, whom we'd yet to meet, joined Captain Buzz on the intercom in the afternoon to provide a series of updates about ship procedures and happenings. Because of his soothing, late-night radio delivery, we started calling him the Voice. A loud tone sounded to get our attention—*bing bong*—and then the Voice echoed through the entire ship.

"Good afternoon, and welcome to your noon announcements," he crooned, though he could have been saying, *You're listening to the Voice, with more music and less talk radio*. . . . If Captain Buzz and the Voice weren't worried, neither were we.

For nearly two weeks we endured clattering silverware and sliding chairs as the waters grew rougher. Just before sunrise on our thirteenth day at sea, about seven hundred miles off the coast of Alaska, as I was deep in an Ambien-induced haze, our ship sailed directly into three major storm systems. Shortly after I awoke, the Voice crackled across the speaker system.

Bing bong.

"Good morning." The Voice sounded as if he hadn't slept all night. "We are encountering severe weather, so we're asking everyone to put on your life jackets and stay in your rooms. We're experiencing extremely large swells, so this is merely a precaution to ensure the safety of all passengers. Once again, we are asking you to put on your life jackets and stay in your rooms."

Jaret and I looked at each other, smiled nervously, and searched the closet for our clunky, neon life jackets. The night we'd left Vancouver, all students had gathered for a drill at our assigned "muster stations," where we'd congregate in the event of an emergency. From there we practiced boarding the lifeboats hooked outside the ship walls. Dressed in our life jackets, we playfully turned on their blinking lights and poked one another, as we struggled to seem cool on the voyage's first night. It was like freshman year all over again, and nobody paid much attention to the instructions we were given.

This time it wasn't a drill, though we still didn't take the instructions seriously. Once Jaret and I strapped on our life jackets, we stood on our mattresses and watched through the porthole window as the waves rose higher and higher. We rode the ship's ebb and flow for an hour, like cowboys straddling a bucking bronco at the state fair—until we felt the entire boat shudder.

"Something's wrong," Jaret said.

We didn't know it yet, but the combined force of the three storms had created a sixty-foot rogue wave that charged across the ocean toward our ship. It smashed into the vessel head-on. And as the wall of water rushed over the bow, it shattered the bulletproof windows of the ship's bridge and flooded the main power supply. The icy water shorted the electronic controls, which caused the engines to die and the navigational equipment to shut down.

Bing bong.

The Voice sounded as if he'd just sprinted a marathon. He gasped for air between each urgent statement.

"Ladies and gentlemen. Get to the fifth floor or higher! Stay out of the elevators. Help the women and children up the stairs. Keep your life jackets on, *and get to your muster stations immediately!*"

I coughed out a single breath as the weight of realization struck my chest. Bile from my stomach rose into my throat, my legs went wobbly, and I lost all strength to stand.

From what I could remember from our drills, the dangling lifeboats were our only way off the ship. Given the conditions, there was no way we could get outside to board them, and any inflatable rafts would flip almost instantly. There was no good plan of escape.

I'm going to die today, I thought. *I'm going to drown in freezing waters within the next two hours.* I was in free fall. How was this possible?

This ship is definitely going down, I thought, *and there's nothing I can do to stop it.* I could feel the panic rising within me. *But why? Is this what my time here was meant for? For me to perish in the middle of the ocean?* I closed my eyes, asked those questions to the higher power I'd always prayed to, and suddenly a wave of calm washed over me.

With 100 percent conviction, I knew that it wasn't my time. It was a feeling unlike anything else I'd ever experienced. With perfect knowledge, I suddenly knew that I had more to do during my time here than to disappear into the frigid waters. "21-Year-Old Perishes at Sea" would not be my story. There would be no candlelight vigils or scholarship funds in my name. I wasn't sure what my purpose was, but I suddenly knew that it both existed and hadn't been fulfilled. As quickly as I thought I'd die, I was now certain that I would survive.

I just had to figure out how.

I looked through the porthole again to see what I was up against. We were nearly seven hundred miles from land, in the North Pacific, in winter—wildly thrashing against the waves. Hypothermia was a given, and one of the few tips I remembered from our drills was to wear warm, long-sleeved clothing if we had to evacuate into water. I threw on my Brown University basketball sweatpants and a hooded sweatshirt to stay warm. Just then, my friends Dave and Reed charged into my room.

Dave's father was a pastor, which made Dave a very, very religious dude. Reed, a Texas native, was a real Southern gentleman. And Jaret was a born-again Christian from Stillwater, Oklahoma. So not only was I in the company of a new band of brothers, but traditional, chivalrous ones at that.

"There's mass hysteria outside, prayer circles, and everyone thinks we're dying," Reed said. He and Dave urged that no matter what happened, it was our duty to put on a strong front as we guided others up the stairs to the fifth and sixth floors.

"No matter how bad it gets," Reed said, "the four of us need to seem totally calm and confident that we'll get through this. People will look to us for direction, so no matter how bad it gets, make sure you put on a strong face."

Before facing the madness in the hall, I changed into a thin, long-sleeved fleece and the only pair of light khaki pants I'd packed. If I wanted to survive, I had to swim; and if I wanted to swim, I couldn't do it in absorbent, heavy sweats.

I looked directly into the mirror, lifting my shirt to reveal the tattoo on my chest. Two years earlier I'd inscribed the words *Ani Ma'amin*, Hebrew for "I believe," in a reverse image over my heart so that I would read them correctly each day in the mirror. They're the first two words in a prayer that assures that if you have lived with the right deeds and actions in this life, you will be rewarded with redemption in the next. When I'd gotten the tattoo, I respected and believed in the power of faith to carry a person through his or her darkest moments, but now my faith in a higher power was truly my only lifeline.

Ani Ma'amin. I repeated the words, praying to those watching over me, and then walked outside to face the hysteria.

I joined Reed, Jaret, and Dave at our posts to help everyone get to higher ground while the boat swayed more violently. Once people were safely upstairs, I climbed to an enclosed area on the sixth floor and sat with my back to the elevators. Two by two, students began clinging to each other in tight bear hugs, hoping that amid the tossing the combined weight of their bodies would keep them in one place. I stayed close to Jaret and Reed as I locked arms with a girl nearby. To my left, a ship worker in his midforties who'd been traveling with the MV *Explorer* for years started hypnotically rocking and crying while clutching his Bible in one hand and rosary beads in the other. *If he's that terrified, this is really bad.* I closed my eyes and rubbed the letters on my chest.

Bing bong.

Captain Buzz. He said we'd need to endure the storm while the crew did its best to compensate for the damage done to the controls, which had shut the engines down. He did not mention that he'd also put out a distress call to the coast guard, and rescue crews were on their way.

Meanwhile, the crying, prayers, and screams continued as we waited for instructions. I stationed myself outside the dining hall.

To keep from moving across the floor, students grabbed on to poles, railings, and each other—hoping the vessel wouldn't capsize entirely. The boat tilted to one side until we were practically parallel with the water, and then did the same on the other, as cutlery and broken dishes screeched ominously across the dining-hall floor. I'm not sure what was more frightening—knowing we were at the mercy of the sea, or watching the portholes fill with water or clouds based on which angle we leaned toward.

After several hours, a group of students decided that we needed to explore how we might abandon this death trap. We knew we had to get the boats down from the davits, which were outside. A wooden door opened to a ten-foot-wide walkway, with a sturdy railing. Maybe if we held on tightly enough, we could make our way to a lifeboat? Someone suggested we try. A shipman cracked the door, and the wind's brute force flung it wide open.

"Close the door! Close the door!" students screamed.

The ship was midtilt as this occurred. We were lifted into the air at a steep incline. The open door hung below us, like a gaping mouth to the deadly waters below. Students began sliding toward the door. If they fell, they'd slip into the freezing ocean waters. The screams got louder.

We grabbed each other to keep from falling, and when the MV *Explorer* rocked back onto her other side, a shipman was able to grab the door handle and close it. We collapsed, exhausted.

After several hours, the tossing eased, and Captain Buzz regained power to the first engine; five hours later, the second one began to work. The engines didn't exactly purr, but the shakes and shudders were progress. We grew optimistic. Ship workers began passing out dinner rolls, and the day-old bread helped settle our stomachs and our nerves. Finally, after we'd spent seven hours in our life vests, the Voice returned.

Bing bong.

"Ladies and gentlemen, it is now safe to return to your rooms. Please be patient with us as we figure out what to do about today's events. The ship is badly damaged, so be careful around broken glass, and please stay tuned for further updates."

Walking back to my room, I surveyed the wreckage in awe and apprehension. Library shelves that once held Frommer's travel guides and atlases of the world were empty or splintered in half. Tables were smashed to pieces, and jagged shards of glass covered the floor. The historic grand piano in the Main Hall had flipped over and shattered.

I had a fleeting vision of the shaken student body rising in mutiny—vandalizing their rooms, calling for Captain Buzz's resignation, and demanding an end to Semester at Sea. Instead the day's events brought us all closer together. Adversity bonds people more often than it breaks them.

Nobody talked much about the storm in the twenty-four hours that followed. We fell into a state of silent introspection. If someone started crying, another would stop to comfort him. Some students quietly self-organized to repair the library and collect the broken glass. Others wrote in their journals or called home on satellite phones to make sure their parents knew they were safe. The following day, I passed two guys playing a board game and heard the person ahead of me say, "Are you fucking kidding me? You're playing Battleship? Seriously?!" I laughed harder than I had in weeks. It was such a relief to let the anxiety go.

Days later we docked in Honolulu, since the engines were too damaged to reach our initial destination of South Korea. As soon as my feet touched land, I dropped to my knees and kissed the hot pavement. My heart leapt at the sight of waving families and beaming hula dancers. I was safe.

But I was also forever altered because I now knew that my life had purpose. Out of catastrophe emerged clarity. When faced with the prospect of death, something deep within me fought back. I was here for a reason. I rubbed my tattoo again, this time in thanks, as the MV *Explorer* bobbed in the distance—battered, but still afloat.

EVERY PENCIL
HOLDS A PROMISE

Through a miraculous effort of administrative coordination, the Semester at Sea front office was able to ensure that our semester abroad wasn't canceled and arranged for us to continue onward while they repaired the MV *Explorer*. As we traveled from one stop to the next, staying in hotels and guesthouses, many of the students collected souvenirs from each country. Some saved shot glasses with the names of cities etched on them in local languages. Others bought a hat or saved a beer bottle. A few took pictures of Beanie Babies in front of famous landmarks. We were college kids, each finding trinkets to document where we'd been and remember something we gained there.

Although I didn't want junky souvenirs, I did want to collect something I could recall and cherish later. Before I got on the ship, I had decided I would ask one child per country, "If you could have anything in the world, what would you want most?" This would give me a chance to connect with at least one kid in every country. I would have the kids write down their answer, and when I returned, I would create a map of their responses. I expected to hear "a flat-screen TV," "an iPod," or "a fast car." I thought I'd gather a series of responses that sounded like the things I wanted as a child—the latest toy, a shiny car, or a big new house.

When an adorable girl in Hawaii approached me and asked if we could be friends, I said yes without hesitation. "But first, I have something very important to ask you," I said. "If you could have anything in the world, what would you want most?"

She put her finger to her chin and glanced knowingly at her mom. "To dance," she replied with a confident nod.

I laughed. "No, I meant if you could have absolutely anything in the entire world, what would it be?"

She smiled, now fully understanding my question. "To dance!" she replied again with delight.

"Wow, that's beautiful," I said with a massive grin. Her answer was disarming in its honesty. I thought back to the happiest moments of my life and realized that many of them involved dancing without any inhibition—at my first Michael Jackson concert, at my dad's surprise fortieth birthday party, at our annual Homecoming Dance, and the list went on. The purest joys are available to all of us, and they're unrelated to status, recognition, or material desires. I clearly had a lot to learn from the unsullied perspective of those I would encounter while traveling, so I decided that for the rest of my trip I would spend more time asking questions than trying to provide answers. Listening intensely is a far more valuable skill than speaking immensely.

In Beijing, I asked a girl near the entrance to the Forbidden Temple what she most wanted in the world, and she said, "A book."

"Really? You can have anything," I urged.

"A book."

Her mother explained that the girl loved school, but didn't have any books of her own. This child's dream was to have something I took for granted every single day.

In Kowloon, Hong Kong, I asked a young boy what he wanted. His older brother translated my question, then translated the response: "Magic."

Alongside the Mekong River in Vietnam I asked a shy six-year-old girl what she would want most. She spoke in a quiet voice as she stared at the muddy, brown soil below. "I want my mom to be healthy. She is sick in bed all day, and I just want her to hold my hand when I walk to school."

Thirty days after we began the trip, I awoke to a blazing red sun rising over the port of Chennai, India. My mind was on getting to Varanasi.

The Ganges River in Varanasi is one of the dirtiest rivers in the world—heavily polluted with industrial and human waste—but is also the most sacred. I'd wanted to walk along its banks ever since I saw that scene in *Baraka*, and the experience with the Wave only heightened my desire. During those long hours when it seemed unclear whether we would survive, I prayed more than I ever had before. The feeling that I had more to do—a purpose—only became more powerful. Now, I just had to find out what exactly it was. I thought I might find some answers at the Ganges, the holiest body of water in Hinduism and one of the most spiritually devout places in the world.

My first night in India, I came down with a terrible fever. By the time we arrived at the airport the next morning, I was covered in a cold sweat and running a 103-degree temperature. I let everyone pass through the security checkpoint while I gathered my strength, afraid that if others knew how sick I was, they wouldn't let me go on the trip. With a heavy backpack on my shoulders, I struggled to see straight, and when it was my turn to walk through the metal detector, I looked down to see my feet zigzagging.

The next thing I knew, I was on my back, looking up at Indian security guards shouting. I had fainted. Two guards each grabbed one of my arms and lifted me. Delirious, I thought they were taking me to prison. Instead they removed my backpack, placed it on the X-ray belt, and walked me through the metal detector. On the other side, they strapped the backpack to my shoulders and pointed me to a boarding gate ahead.

When I arrived at the gate, another student came over and shouted, "Where were you? The whole group was looking everywhere for you! And what's up with your face? You look like a ghost. You're sweating through your shirt."

I told him I had just fainted. "Don't tell anyone," I pleaded. Nothing was going to stop me from getting to Varanasi. Because I was so sick, I decided I would cleanse myself in the Ganges when we got there. I figured I couldn't feel any worse, so the holy waters could only help.

In the days that followed, my fever abated. At night we went to the train station outside the city of Agra, where I witnessed something I had never before seen in my life: hordes of barefoot children, covered in dirt from head to toe, begging for money and food. They were so incredibly young to be alone. I saw four-year-olds begging with six-month-olds in their arms. The pain on their faces was devastating.

We were forewarned that giving child beggars money makes them effective workers for the gang lords that put them on the streets and perpetuates the cycle that keeps them there. Some of us bought the children food to eat, but we still felt helpless and dejected. I didn't know how to help. I stayed up the entire night thinking about what I'd seen.

The next morning we went to Agra Fort, a stunning red temple within view of the Taj Mahal. But I couldn't pay attention to the architecture around me. My mind kept returning to thoughts about the children begging on the street, and I decided that I would ask one of them my question. They had absolutely nothing. If they could have anything, what would they want most?

I strayed away from my group and found a young boy with big brown eyes who was previously begging, but now sat alone. As I approached him to talk, a man came over to translate. I explained that I had a question for the boy. I was asking one child per country, if the child could have anything in the world, what would it be? I wanted to know, what would the boy want if he could have any one thing? He thought about it for a few seconds, then responded confidently:

"A pencil."

"Are you sure?" I asked. He had no family, nothing, yet his request was so basic.

More men came over and started chiming in. They prodded him, "You can have anything. He might give it to you!"

The boy remained constant with his wish: "A pencil."

I had a No. 2 yellow pencil in my backpack. I pulled it out and handed it to him.

As it passed from my hand to his, his face lit up. He looked at it as if it were a diamond. The men explained that the boy had never been to school, but he had seen other children writing with pencils. It shocked me that he had never once been to school. It then started to settle in that this was the reality for many children across the world. Could something as small as a pencil, the foundation of an education, unlock a child's potential?

For me that pencil was a writing utensil, but for him it was a key. It was a symbol. It was a portal to creativity, curiosity, and possibility. Every great inventor, architect, scientist, and mathematician began as a child holding nothing more than a pencil. That single stick of wood and graphite could enable him to explore worlds within that he would never otherwise access.

Up until that point, I had always thought that I was too young to make a difference. I had been told that without the ability to make a large donation to a charity, I couldn't help change someone's life. But through the small act of giving one child one pencil, that belief was shattered. I realized that even big waves start with small ripples. *This is my thing*, I thought. *Rather than offering money or nothing at all, I'm going to give kids pencils and pens as I travel.*

The next day we headed to Varanasi with the dozens of other students on the five-day tour, and several chaperoning professors in their fifties and sixties. We arrived in Varanasi during Shivratri, the festival that celebrates the Hindu deity Shiva, "the Transformer." Hundreds of thousands had descended on the city for this holy event. We planned to take a sunset tour first, then a sunrise tour the next morning, during which we would see people burning bodies on the Ganges. Our guide, Vanay, was extremely spiritual, and during the sunset tour he explained that cremation on the banks of the Ganges allowed direct access to nirvana in the afterlife. But riverside cremation was expensive, and most could not afford the full ceremony—the poor often wrapped their dead loved ones in cloth and floated them down the river. We would see all of this the following morning.

The group that had visited the day before had sent us beautiful pictures from the banks of the river illuminated by glowing candles, but I didn't want to experience it just behind the lens of a camera. I wanted to submerge myself in it. I wanted to bathe in the water as the locals did.

I asked Vanay, "How dirty is it?"

"Biologically, it is very dirty," he said. "But if it is holy, and I believe this is the water of G-d, why would G-d hurt me?"

Vanay then reached down, scooped the river water into his hands, and drank a mouthful. Jaws dropped all around the boat. Inside, I was beaming. I had found a kindred spirit.

At dinner that night, I quietly told a few friends that I was going into the Ganges the next morning during our sunrise tour. Word spread quickly, and one of the chaperones approached me. "We will not allow it," he said. "You will get extremely ill if you go in the water and possibly catch a parasite that will kill you. You absolutely cannot go in."

I told him I respected his advice, but would make the decision for myself.

The next morning I woke up and got dressed with shorts under my jeans so I could jump into the river at the appropriate moment. I saw the chaperone again, and he reminded me, "If you go in, I will not let you back on the bus." His wife, also a professor, chimed in, "This is dangerous. If you get sick from the water, which you will, we're going to leave you behind."

"I don't want to be rude, but you are not my parents," I said forcefully.

Before we boarded the bus, Vanay approached me. "Many people are concerned. I hear you want to go in the water. Why?"

"It's the holiest body of water on earth," I replied, feeling a bit like a broken record. "I want to say my prayers and meditations in one of the places that I believe is closest to G-d. I might not be a Hindu, but any place that others pray to so fervently, in my mind, is sacred."

He put his hand on my shoulder. "This is very good. But don't just jump in. . . . I will show you where to enter after the tour."

My heart leapt. I had an ally.

During the sunrise tour we saw people of all ages bathing in the river. One man did a floating meditation, another taught his children the morning rituals.

When we arrived back on the shore, as the group took pictures of the surrounding buildings, Vanay nodded toward me and pointed at a few steps that led into the water. I discreetly walked to the side and stripped down to my shorts. I walked down to the bank and into the river. I dunked my whole body, and without thinking about it, I submerged my head and opened my mouth, letting the water rush in the way I usually do in a bathtub or pool. I rose to the top and spit it out without even thinking about the mistake I may have made taking in the world's holiest—and biologically dirtiest—water. No turning back now.

Once I was shoulder deep in the water, I closed my eyes and said my prayers. As I emerged from the water ten minutes later, an elderly shaman with a saffron robe and orange turban filled with a cascade of white hair called out to me, "Why go in the Ganga?"

I told him why and he took my hand in his. He pulled out a ball of bright red and yellow string and looped the string twice around my wrist. He closed his eyes and recited a prayer of protection and goodwill, then told me this was a holy string of Varanasi.

A small crowd of Indian boys gathered around us. We walked together for a few blocks, but before they departed, they asked me for some money to help them. Instead, I reached into my pocket and pulled out a few pencils. I gave one to each of the boys. The change in them was immediate. They began drawing on pieces of paper a shop owner gave them and practiced their letters for others to see. They had a new sense of freedom, a new independence. I was moved by how such a small act could open up a sense of possibility, wonder, and connection in those who had so little. Ideas began to percolate in my mind, but I forced myself not to get too excited. No matter how hard I tried, though, I couldn't get the image of that boy holding that pencil out of my head.

DO THE SMALL THINGS
THAT MAKE OTHERS FEEL BIG

After India we traveled the open plains of the Kenyan Masai Mara, spent time in the townships of South Africa, and explored the overgrown favelas of Brazil. Rather than pursuing guided tours at historic sites, I developed a habit of befriending locals who were my age and asking if I could spend time in their home villages. This simple request took me far off the beaten path and enabled me to gain an inside glimpse into how rural communities functioned. I became obsessed with learning how other people lived and was consumed by a newfound passion to help. By the time Semester at Sea came to a close, we had circled the globe and I felt like a man on fire.

When we arrived at the docks in Ft. Lauderdale where our families awaited us, I was immediately struck by how much bigger Americans were than the people I'd met abroad. It was so rare to see an overweight person in the developing world, yet more than half of the people waving from the Floridian shores seemed enormous. As Marcel Proust wrote, "The real voyage of discovery consists not in seeking new landscapes but in having new eyes." Although I had been worried about experiencing culture shock in foreign countries throughout the trip, the greatest culture shock was about to occur back home.

Ma was eager to take me to her golf club in Boca Lago and fill me with heaping plates of brisket, meatballs, gefilte fish, sushi, and chicken-noodle soup—delicacies after months on the ship eating stale rolls and soggy salad. I wanted to enjoy it, but as we scraped the excess into the trash, all I could think about was how many people went to sleep hungry in the places I'd just visited.

That night my brother, Scott, who had become the top night-club promoter in Atlanta, insisted that we go clubbing in South Beach to celebrate my return. I hadn't even been back on US soil for more than ten hours, but we went to the Miami hot spot Sky-bar. Beautiful, scantily dressed women waved sparklers and danced around carrying enormous $5,000 bottles of Dom Pérignon. Their performance eerily resembled the religious ceremonies I had seen over the past few months, but in the Candomblé ceremonies of Brazil and Cao Dai temples of Vietnam, people were celebrating life, not bottles of alcohol. I could feel myself judging those around me, which wasn't fair because they hadn't seen what I'd seen, nor had I lived a day in their shoes.

No matter how hard I tried, though, I knew that this feeling wouldn't go away until I traveled again. I had grown so much in my time abroad, but it seemed as if life at home had pretty much stayed the same. It felt as if I were back in my childhood bedroom; I knew everything so well that I could find the light switch in the dark, but I no longer fit in the surroundings once everything was illuminated. My parents had always told me that when it came to travel "we'll support you, just not financially," so I hatched a plan to get back on the open road.

After working multiple jobs through May and June, I had enough money to backpack on a shoestring budget through July and August. With my friend Luke, I started in Europe, where we lived on cheap sandwiches in well-traveled tourist hot spots like Paris, Vienna, and Prague. But we also visited more remote cities like Bratislava, Slovakia, and Split, Croatia, just to chase adventures off the beaten path. In these distant locations we often met the kindest people, who took us into their homes. In Dubrovnik, Croatia, we stayed with an elderly couple we met at the bus station. After telling them how much we missed homemade breakfasts, they placed warm bread, scrambled eggs, and fresh-squeezed juice in the kitchen for us each morning. These treats lifted our spirits and reminded us that even on the road you can find strangers who can make you feel like family. The food was certainly delicious, but the gesture showed us that kindness cannot be evaluated in dollars and cents. The only way to measure it is in the weight of compassion that the act itself carries forward into the life of another.

Following my time in Europe, I spent the rest of the summer backpacking through Singapore, Thailand, and Cambodia with my SAS friend Dennis and his college roommate, Zach. The futuristic feel of Singapore and gorgeous beaches of Thailand did not disappoint. In Cambodia, we were hosted by Scott Neeson, a tough-willed Australian and a former film executive who oversaw the release of some of the top movies of all time, including *Titanic* and *X-Men*.

A few years before, Scott had visited Steung Meanchey, a notorious garbage dump in Phnom Penh, where several thousand of the region's poorest kids were living in squalor. After recognizing that his help wasn't doing enough from afar, Scott walked away from his life in Hollywood. He sold his house and Porsche and moved alone to Cambodia to create the Cambodian Children's Fund (CCF), which provides housing, education, food, and life-skills training for kids in the most impoverished communities.

The organization was small, nimble, and run by someone I deeply connected with. On several occasions I walked with Scott through Steung Meanchey. The smells of garbage were overwhelming, but everyone seemed to know him, and he chatted with multiple families about the need to bring their children to the CCF for medical attention. The services he provided were to children who desperately needed help, and he had a personal relationship with those he looked to support.

He explained that he had a staff of local Cambodians, which was best for the children they supported, but he needed help raising funds back in the States. I immediately agreed to become the Cambodian Children's Fund's first fundraising coordinator and vowed to devote my senior year of college to helping the organization educate more children.

Since I was born on Halloween, I planned out the costume party I had always hosted for my birthday, but this time I asked for a $10 donation at the door in lieu of gifts. The party raised several thousand dollars and would be the first of many events I'd host to support the CCF.

Although the first party was a success, I ran into a roadblock when planning the next event. I had no proof that I was affiliated with the CCF, so I couldn't get nonprofit discounts on venues I tried to rent. When I asked Scott for a way to acknowledge my association, he mailed me my own two-sided business cards. On one side it listed my name and "Fundraising Coordinator" in English, and on the other side it was translated into Khmer, the native language of Cambodia.

It was such a small thing, but those business cards were the best gift I'd ever received. I felt that I belonged. I felt that I mattered. The $20 investment it took to produce those business cards gave me a sense of value and enabled me to raise thousands of dollars for the CCF over the next few years. I suddenly had an identity that I could be proud of, and all it took was a piece of paper.

Although I had a sharper sense of purpose than ever before, I still had this lingering feeling that no one understood me. I'd gone through such a rapid and profound transformation over my four years of college, and sometimes I felt as though my life was trailing far behind where my mind was taking me. When I hatched plans to launch a nonprofit after graduation, my parents, professors, and peers all tried to dissuade me. I'd worked hard to complete a triple major in economics, sociology, and public and private sector organizations, and they didn't want me to squander it. "You should go work at the highest levels in business," they said. "This way you can make as much money as possible and then use those dollars in your forties or fifties to fund something that will better the world."

Reluctantly, I decided to follow their rationale. I knew my résumé was strong enough to open a lot of doors, and I began applying to the most lucrative jobs that a recent graduate could attain. But I knew that deep inside I was now driven by something completely different.

The spare cash I'd earned through the jobs I'd held over the years had allowed me to accumulate some savings, but whenever I looked into my wallet, the single most important item in there was always my CCF business card. It meant so much more to me than the dollar bills it rested beside because it enabled me to belong to something bigger than myself. Purpose can manifest from so many different places, but it most often appears through the small things that enable us to feel connected to a broader whole.

Although I was about to plunge into the corporate sector, my CCF business cards unlocked a feeling that I wanted to explore further. I decided to take one more big trip into the developing world. I had my backpack, a pair of aviators, and enough cash to last four months in Latin America.

The only thing left to do was to write a will and hop on a plane heading south.

Mantra 6

TOURISTS SEE, TRAVELERS SEEK

I can't explain exactly why I did it, but rationally, or irrationally, I just decided that it had to be done. I was twenty-three years old and I wrote a will.

I didn't have much: my music went to my sister, journals to my brother, and any money I'd made went to the Cambodian Children's Fund. I typed up the document after dinner the night before I left and asked my mother to sign as a witness.

As she held the pen to sign my will, balancing against the wooden kitchen counter, tears started to stream down her cheeks. "You're really making me do this?" she pleaded. I nodded. I was about to travel alone through a remote part of the world for months, and I wanted to make sure the right people got my possessions in case something happened. I knew my belongings weren't of immense worth, but they were important to me. Sometimes you have to leave things behind to understand their true value.

Over dinner, my dad had asked me for my itinerary. I couldn't help but laugh. He repeated, "I'm not messing around. I want to know where you're going to be each of the first thirteen days. You don't have to tell me where you're staying, but I want the names of the towns and cities."

"Dad, I don't know where I'm staying the first night, so how can I possibly tell you where I'm staying for the next twelve?" I told him of a place called Semuc Champey, which my SAS roommate Jaret had traveled to last year. It had natural, emerald-green pools and a cave you could swim through for miles by holding a candle to light the way. "I'll go find Semuc Champey first—it's somewhere north of Guatemala City—and then explore Central and South America from there. That's really the only plan that I have."

"And Matt's okay with this too?"

My childhood friend Matt and I were supposed to travel together for the first two months, but now it looked as if he might join for a week or two about a month into the trip. "He actually just emailed me some bad news tonight. I don't know if he's flying out with me tomorrow morning."

"Is that a joke?"

"No. Trust me, I'm not happy about it either. But at least at some point in the next few days I'll be in Semuc Champey. It's supposedly incredible."

"Show it to me in the guidebook."

"I told you already. I'm not bringing a guidebook."

My dad couldn't take it anymore. "What the hell does that mean that you're not bringing a guidebook!" he screamed. "Are you purposely trying to piss me off?"

I inhaled deeply and curled my toes into the soles of my sneakers. "That's not how I travel anymore. I'm going to rely on the advice of the travelers and locals that I meet along the way. I'll make my itinerary as I go." I heard the words come out of my mouth with all of the naive confidence that a twenty-three-year-old could muster.

Staring back at me, furiously biting his lower lip to contain his anger, my dad shook his head in disbelief. "Just make damn sure you stay safe," he said. "And remember, Dad's Rules."

As I sat on the flight from New York City to Guatemala City, I kept picturing my mother signing my will, and it left me with a pounding sense of mortality. It's not that I thought the plane would crash or that my journey would end in some catastrophic way. It was that I was about to travel completely alone for the very first time. SAS and the subsequent travels were eye-opening experiences, but I had always traveled in small groups with friends. Now, I was my only guide.

When I arrived in Guatemala City, I immediately caught a local bus to see the emerald pools of Semuc Champey. They were even more gorgeous than I expected, as were the towering Mayan temples of Tikal in northern Guatemala.

Next I went to the riverside town of Río Dulce. When I bought my bus ticket in Flores, a group of six tattooed teenagers in white tank tops hassled me for money. I acted as if I didn't speak Spanish. *"No hablo español,"* I said in my most American accent, not revealing that I actually understood every word they said. They snickered to each other, and when we boarded the bus, they positioned themselves in seats around me.

Each began describing the items of mine they would steal. *I want his watch. I get his passport. I'm keeping his wallet.* Over the next seven hours I didn't get up from my seat once. Once the sun fell and the bus got dark, I discreetly pulled my feet out of my shoes and stuffed my wallet and passport in opposite sneakers so I could hide them by standing on them. When we finally arrived at the Río Dulce stop, I glanced at the boys seated around me. Each was fast asleep. I quietly slipped off the bus, into the pouring rain, and heaved a sigh of relief. It was nearly 1:00 a.m., and I needed to find a place to sleep.

After walking down several shady alleys in search of lodging, my passport and money still tucked deeply into my shoes, I met a man who offered me a taxi ride to a hostel five miles away. He pointed to a nice car, which I assumed was his cab, and we negotiated a fair price. But then he led me to a beat-up car with busted windows on an empty side street. Something told me that driving into the dark with this stranger was a bad idea. I quickly began walking away, and within seconds he started screaming at me. I watched as he ran to the passenger side of the car and reached into the glove box. He pulled out a handgun.

I ran. As I sprinted through the rain, my heart thumped loudly in my ears. One hundred fifty feet away was an iron-gated hotel. I pounded on the gate for the night guard to let me in. The buzzer sounded just as I turned around to see the man with the gun about thirty feet behind me. I ran inside, booked a room (even though the guy behind the counter charged me double at that late hour), and stayed up all night replaying what had happened over and over in my head. Spiders crawled the walls around me, and for the first time I began to doubt why I had ever left home.

I'd never been so far removed, physically and emotionally, from everything that made me happy. I felt completely alone. But I knew that once I made it through the night, things would get better. They say that the darkest moment in the night is when the stars shine their brightest. That night in Río Dulce felt awfully dark, but when your faith is tested you simply have to believe that there will be light ahead and continue moving forward.

Several days later I arrived at Lake Atitlán, where I decided to spend nearly a month at Las Pirámides, a center for spirituality and meditation. Every morning a group of twenty travelers would wake up at 6:30 a.m. to watch the sun rise over the three volcanoes and then attend classes on yoga, meditation, and mystical teachings throughout the day. We each stayed in our own small wooden hut with a pyramid-shaped roof (hence the name Las Pirámides) and cooked three meals together every day. I had never lived such a basic, healthy lifestyle, and I discovered a calming clarity in the slow passing of each day. I found myself strangely excited for the final week's commitment to five days of absolute silence. The center's founder, Chati, had been teaching us about the concept of spiritual guides, and I yearned for the quiet time to reflect on who those people may have been in my life thus far.

Matt had finally arrived, and in preparation for our days of silence we headed out to Las Cristalinas, a small lakefront area where we could catch up and relax. As we rode on the back of a pickup truck with local families, the sun baked our shoulders. After swimming in the crystal waters, Matt left me alone to get an ice cream nearby. I was writing a few thoughts in my leather-bound journal when a small Guatemalan man in his midforties interrupted me.

"Hello, how are you?" he asked, speaking in broken English. "My name is Joel Puac. What is your name?" He pronounced the words slowly, as if he had been preparing them for weeks.

Normally I would have asked to be left alone, but I had recently adopted the mantra "Tourists see, travelers seek." I was a traveler, one who sought to experience more than just churches and museums. I wanted to see each country through a local's eyes, and something about the humility in this man's voice made me curious. I told him my name was Adam and asked him what brought him to the lakefront that day. He was there to celebrate the baptism of his grandchild, he said. After ten minutes of standard conversation, he explained why he had approached me.

"I am a teacher. I teach myself English, but my pronunciation is not so good. I would like you to help me learn English, so I can teach my children. I would like to invite you to stay in my village. You can stay as long as you want with me and my wife."

"How far away do you live?" I asked, half joking.

"Two hours, into the mountains. My village is called Palestina. I give you my mobile number and you call me when you want to come." He was dead serious.

I was blown away by this unexpected offer, but I needed more information. My family would want to know where I was headed. "If I decide to stay with you, what is the street name and number of your home?"

"Our streets have no names. The houses have no numbers. Just ask for Joel in Palestina. It is a very small village. The people know me."

He then extended a small, leathery hand. I could tell that this man farmed his own land to feed his family. We shook as he nodded firmly, then left me there to ponder whether I would accept his offer.

Moments later, Matt returned with a big smile. "I finally found a place with ice cream. Sorry it took so long. Did I miss anything?"

That night I couldn't sleep. I considered the possibility that Joel had appeared in my life for a distinct reason and recognized that at the very least this man could be a guide of some sort.

For his part, hosting me could change the future for his children and grandchildren. He saw me as a window to a larger world—his family could learn a bit of English and gain a broader global perspective that could motivate them to pursue life outside their tiny village.

Joel reminded me of my late grandfather Apu, the rock of my entire family. Apu had the strength to survive the Holocaust, the faith to find my grandmother, and the fortitude to leave his native country and bring my family to the United States—to give us the opportunity for a better life. I had looked to Apu for guidance my whole childhood when he was alive, and through my prayers after he passed away. In those prayers I often asked him to send me a sign or a messenger, and if there was even a chance that Joel was that person, I had to follow through with his offer.

For years I had struggled with intense feelings of guilt. I was born into the lottery of life with a winning ticket—a loving family, great education, good health. But what had I done to deserve any of it? Why was I born into those blessings when so many others were born into suffering? Why was I born into a booming city when others are born into villages without electricity or water in war-torn nations? I was reluctant to admit it, but I felt that I owed something to those who were less fortunate, because in my mind I had never done anything to earn the good fortune I enjoyed.

Yet in hearing Joel's request, and how his dream was to educate his kids and grandkids and great-grandkids to ensure a better way of life for them, I was reminded that my good fortune was the product of many long, laborious, and often tragic years. I was the result of Apu's dream. I was the result of the sacrifices each of my ancestors made so that I could live out the life they never had. And they would want nothing more than for me to fully realize what they worked so hard for and to pass on the gifts I'd received. Through Joel, I had an opportunity to honor them.

I knew if Joel's grandson grew up and felt guilt over the sacrifices

made for him, it would be a slap in the face to Joel and everything
he did with such pure intention. My sense of guilt and obligation
diminished the hard work and desires of those who came before
me. It was a total emotional shift. Rather than motivation through
obligation, I now felt motivation to celebrate those before me in
a different way. I had a chance to honor Apu by providing greater
opportunity to others.

Six days later, I was on my way to Joel's village, bumping along
dirt roads in a microbus filled with local Guatemalan families.
Two farmers smiled silver-capped-toothed grins at me. To my
left a baby cried on his mother's lap and to my right an elderly
man gripped his field machete tightly. Although my friends at Las
Pirámides thought I was crazy to head into the mountains alone
where I might never return, I trusted Joel and knew this was the
kind of experience I was seeking.

True to Joel's description, Palestina had no street signs or house
numbers. When I asked a local woman for Joel Puac, she pointed
down a long dirt road. *"Todo derecho,"* she said, *straight ahead.* A
neighbor pointed me to Joel's home, and upon my arrival he introduced me to his dogs, chickens, and his ancient father, who lived in
a one-room house next door. Though the old man was hunched,
he clenched my hands with tight, clawlike fingers and led me, the
first American he'd ever met, into his home to show me a treasured
relic. He slowly wiped away the dust on a framed photo: a black-
and-white aerial view of New York City. A friend of his had given
it to him. The Twin Towers had fallen six years earlier, but in the
photo they still dominated the skyline.

Joel showed me around the house: a broken toilet, a small
fridge. He then showed me where I would sleep: a single bed on
one side of a small room. He and his wife, Aurelia, would sleep in
the double bed on the other side of the same room.

"We should start," Joel said abruptly, and placed a small, red plastic table in front of me. On it was an English Bible, a Spanish-English dictionary, and a large cassette recorder. Joel spoke intently of the human need for spirituality. He told me of the issues facing Guatemala and the dangers of Guatemala City. He showed me a scar on his abdomen where he was recently stabbed by vagrants at a nearby market and told me how many people watched it happen but no one did anything.

To teach English to his family, he needed to learn the proper pronunciation, so he used the text he knew best: the Bible. We started at the beginning of the book of Proverbs. He asked me to read aloud into his old-school cassette recorder. He then detailed his plan to listen to the recordings of my voice every evening, saying the words in English, again and again.

Over three days, I spent as much time as I could, legs crossed on the dusty floor, reading into that tape recorder, in the room where we all slept. The space was small and the lights were dim, but the room was vibrant in detail: turquoise and yellow walls decorated with cartoon characters, old calendar cutouts, and pictures of faraway places from magazines. Each afternoon Joel and I made sure the cassettes played back properly. As we listened to my voice crackling through the ancient tape player, I couldn't help but laugh at the beautiful irony of a Jew reading the Christian Bible aloud in a town called Palestina.

Joel had a tiny TV, and at night we would watch movies. It was March, but one night *Elf* was on. We laughed hysterically at the dialogue spoken in Spanish, but Joel focused on the English sub-titles. After the movie, he listened to the day's recordings through his oversize headphones. Hearing him whisper each of the words my voice was speaking into his ears gave me goose bumps. When Joel caught me smiling, he smiled back and said, "I don't want handouts. I want to teach myself, so that when you leave, I can teach my children and the others in my village."

I'd always operated under the vague notion that charitable work was about giving aid to the poor. In Western culture, we are taught that those of us with ample resources and money should share our prosperity with those who have less. I'd thought of charity as a simple transaction, a one-way street.

Joel taught me that my assumptions about the nature of charity had been wrong. When we give handouts to those in poverty, we do them a disservice. We create a cruel cycle of dependence. After three days with Joel in his remote village, I left knowing that he now had tools to self-educate. By listening to that portable tape recorder each night, he would learn to speak a new language. More important, he could share his English skills with his family in the years ahead without relying on the assistance of others.

My experience with Joel sparked a new curiosity within me. As I traveled on twelve-hour overnight buses through Peru, Bolivia, Ecuador, Colombia, Argentina, Chile, and several other countries during the next three months of backpacking, the pencils I handed to children allowed me to ask their parents what they would want most in the world if they could have anything as well. Though I expected to hear "less corrupt government," "new roads," or "a better job," I was met with the same answer nearly every time: "An education for my child." It was the same dream Joel had doggedly pursued and the same one Apu had before him.

At the greatest levels of affluence, and the deepest levels of poverty, parents share the same desire for their children to have a better future. The willingness to sacrifice their own well-being for the betterment of their children is the common thread I witnessed across mothers and fathers from vastly different cultures. And yet, the playing field remains completely uneven.

During those four months in Central and South America, I thought often about Joel. Each night, as I tossed and turned in search of sleep, I wondered if he was sitting up in his bed listening to those cassette tapes. He showed me the essence of leadership by forging into the unknown so that others could follow. He taught me to approach each new person I met with the dignity he or she deserves. And he proved once and for all that Will Ferrell is funny in every single language.

On our last morning together I promised Joel and his father that I would return one day. Perhaps I could start something in the future that would support their region in Guatemala. I explained to them that at the end of my journey throughout Latin America, New York City awaited. I'd trade backpacks and buses for skyscrapers and subway rides.

The city that never sleeps was about to add one more nightwalker to its masses.

ASKING FOR PERMISSION
IS ASKING FOR DENIAL

B ain & Company, the consulting firm that had just offered me a dream job and FedExed a contract that I had yet to sign, flew me and more than twenty other prospects to New York City, put us up in fancy hotels, and invited us to an opulent weekend of extravagant events to learn more about the company and ideally commit to working there. The capstone affair was on Saturday night, a private dinner at BLT Fish, one of the hottest restaurants in the Meatpacking District. I traded my T-shirt and shorts for a dress shirt and slacks and congregated with other prospects on the top floor, where we gathered to accept our job offers in front of the company's most esteemed partners.

The scene looked much like you'd imagine Wall Street did in the 1980s, with top-shelf liquor and flowing champagne. Periodically throughout the meal, the head of recruitment stood up and honored the individuals who had already committed to Bain.

"From Harvard, congratulations to Steven Thompson. From Princeton, a warm welcome to Maria Akadia," she shouted as she handed out bottles of champagne to each new official employee. "Anyone else want to commit?"

Well-dressed soon-to-be college graduates rose out of their seats, declaring, "I'll commit!" More champagne bottles popped, and everyone in the room cheered. The Bain employees at my table watched me closely as the other prospects rose from their seats, one after another.

I had decided that I would pick Bain over my other offers, but like most of the people there, I waited for the ceremonial dinner to make it official. Toward the end, I stood up to announce that I would join as well. Cheers went up from across the room, and a flute of golden champagne was placed in my hand. The whole scene felt foreign, but it felt good.

In the months leading up to this dinner, I had been operating on a tight budget, which had me staying in youth hostels abroad and eating a diet of ramen noodles. But tonight I was enjoying a fantastic steak I didn't have to pay for. It was the best food I'd had in months.

I was sitting to the right of Bain NY's youngest female partner, and I noticed that although she ordered the filet mignon, she didn't touch it; she only ate the vegetables. I had finished mine within five minutes, but her perfect steak remained untouched. Perhaps the alcohol emboldened me to get a little too comfortable, but when she waved her hand for the server to clear her plate and went back to her conversation with the person on her left, I discreetly stabbed her steak with my fork and placed it on my plate.

Yes, it was an idiot move. And apparently I wasn't discreet at all. "Did you just take my steak?" she asked, turning to face me.

The entire table—partners and prospective colleagues—looked

at me. Someone else echoed incredulously, "Seriously? Did you just take her steak?"

My face filled with prickly heat. I could feel myself turning bright red. "I'm sorry," I stammered. I definitely shouldn't have had that last glass of champagne. Or the one before it. "I've been backpacking for so long and this is just too good to let it go to waste. I don't know what I was thinking, but that was totally inappropriate. I'm so sorry."

"Well, now you have to eat it," said the partner across the table, smiling. For the next several minutes, everyone's eyes remained fixed on me as I polished off my second steak of the evening. It was as delicious as the first, but I felt the dissonance between backpacking culture and corporate privilege with each bite. One thing was clear: if I was going to do well at this company, I needed to change more than just my clothes.

I was ecstatic to land the Bain offer, but accepting it had not been an easy decision. The best firms decide on candidates during the same few weeks each fall, and I'd been through interviews with five investment banks, five consulting firms, and one private equity shop during two frantic, rapid-fire weeks.

At my Goldman Sachs interview they asked questions designed to rattle me. "What's the sum of all the numbers between one and one hundred?" they asked on a whim (answer: 5,050). Blackstone Private Equity had eight different employees put me through the wringer, requesting that I build balance sheets and financial models from scratch. When I thought I'd crushed my interviews at a boutique consulting firm that I'd viewed as my "safety" job, they called to tell me that I didn't impress them whatsoever.

I began to understand clearly that I could never make assumptions about how others perceive me. Each day several doors closed, and others opened, some more promising than others. First rounds became second rounds, which became final rounds, but nothing was guaranteed until I had an offer in hand.

After I completed the interviews and returned home, I waited nervously to hear back from each company. I received a call from Bain (my top choice) the day before my birthday. After several white-knuckled minutes of small talk, they made an official job offer, and along with the contract, they sent a massive chocolate cake with the Bain logo and "Happy Birthday Adam" written in frosting on top. It was a terrific birthday present and I was thrilled, but I also received an offer from Lehman Brothers in its esteemed investment bank division.

Lehman was appealing since the pay as an investment banker was considerably higher, but the drawback was that it would require me to work like a dog. While the hours in consulting weren't insubstantial—I was told I'd be in the office from 9:00 a.m. to 9:00 p.m.—the hours in banking were more demanding, and all the first-year investment bankers I knew hated their jobs. At Lehman I would learn how to manage capital but at Bain I would learn how to manage the operations of a company. My plan was to take one of these jobs for a few years and then go to a hedge fund or private equity shop, where the real money was. Once I had a deep enough bank account, I could go off to start my dream non-profit organization. But first I needed money and I needed experience, which meant I planned to work in finance for the next fifteen to twenty years.

I hoped that one of my mentors who ran a successful financial-management firm, George Stanton, could help me make the right decision.

"There actually will be times in life when you should choose money over experience," he said with a stern voice, "but make that choice when the margin is much bigger, when the margin is millions of dollars, not thousands. Although fifty thousand dollars is a lot of money to you right now, in the grand scheme of things, experience will be much more valuable in the long run."

George's advice rang in my ears that night at BLT Fish when I committed to Bain. I decided I would view my time at the company as a form of paid business school. They could work me as hard as they wanted, as long as I learned along the way. Compensation comes in many forms, and if you define your expectations up front, you'll gain far more than just money from the jobs you take.

After several weeks of rigorous training, my first project was to help design the real estate growth strategy for a well-known retailer. I ended up working for the partner whose steak I stole. Fortunately, she laughed about it at our first meeting. "It was a bold move. Ridiculous, but bold too," she teased.

The work at Bain was intriguing during the first few months because the learning curve was so steep. The training was intense and I was gaining new skills that I knew would be valuable throughout my career. Building financial models and impressive PowerPoint presentations was fun at the outset, but by the end of my first year I couldn't look at Excel spreadsheets for twelve hours a day and not lose my mind—so I found other ways to make the environment more entertaining.

As a middle child I'd honed my skills as a prankster, and this became my calling at the company. I would fill the printer with pink paper, turn my coworkers' cubicles into newspaper-covered forts, and constantly mess with my closest friend, Priya. I'd fill her gloves with paper clips, reverse everything on her desk to create a mirror image of how it was supposed to look, and place face lotion on her phone headset before calling her extension.

Although I genuinely liked the people I worked with, I lacked passion for the work itself. I couldn't get excited about making credit-card companies more money by reevaluating their customer-acquisition process, investigating long-term disability insurance for insurance giants, and so forth. As an associate consultant, my job included taking notes in client meetings. In the first few months I diligently recorded the statements of the attendees, but soon I found myself nodding apathetically while writing personal journal entries in my spiral notebook. I scribbled, *I wish I was more interested in this work, but it's just not for me. Find your passion, and you'll find your strength.*

Instead, I spent my first year in New York City drinking and chasing girls. I went out partying five to six nights per week, every single week. I'd often guzzle ten to fifteen drinks in a night, bouncing from bars to clubs until sunrise—whatever it took to get me to feel happy, free, and alive.

I began to detest putting on my consultant's outfit of slacks and a tucked-in button-down. I felt as if I were wearing someone else's uniform. When it came to my year-end review, I was told that my work was error-free and my contributions to the team were valued, but there was a major issue. I looked as if I didn't care in client meetings.

I shrugged off the review and told them that I would try harder. But I knew it was a lie, just as they did.

A little more than a year into my job at Bain, in September 2008, Lehman Brothers declared bankruptcy. What would have happened if I'd gone right instead of left and chosen Lehman over Bain? The offer that appeared financially better ended up being far less secure. I realized how easily material things could be taken away. I really began to evaluate what I was doing. I was partying nearly every night. When my doctor asked me how many drinks I consumed per week, I answered honestly, guessing about fifty. He looked up from his clipboard in shock. "Are you kidding? You're going to kill yourself if you keep this up!"

I recognized that my liver couldn't sustain my drinking habit much longer. Worse, when I evaluated my life, I didn't like whom I had become. I was completely self-absorbed, only chasing things that benefited me personally. I hadn't done anything truly nice for anyone else since I'd moved to New York. Although I lived in a beautiful apartment and had access to parties, girls, and everything I thought I desired, I felt empty and awful inside.

When I sat with my parents, I told them, "I want to work on things that I'm more passionate about."

"You can't. First you need real-world experience," they said. I was on a safe path to financial security, and they didn't want me off it.

"But I don't feel like myself," I complained.

"That's what it means to do a job!" yelled my dad. "Grow up, and stop being such a baby."

He was right. It was time to grow up. A few months before, one of the world's leading nonprofit foundations became a pro bono client at Bain, and I politely emailed the manager running the case to ask if I could join her team. She didn't select me, and probably with good reason. During the annual company meeting, it was announced in front of every partner and manager that I was voted "Most likely to be sleeping in the wellness room," which everyone knew was the spot for a nap after a big night out. The award itself was a playful gag, but it was a wake-up call for me about the reputation I was building within the company.

I clearly needed to change things fast, and I couldn't do so by waiting around for someone else to clean up my act. I needed to take charge of my own fate. I started by focusing on my health, spending less time at bars and a lot more time at the gym. My energy levels increased, and I found myself feeling more confident and alert in meetings. When another opportunity arose to work on a case with the leading nonprofit delivering poverty services within New York City, this time I didn't ask.

I sought out the person managing the case, my friend Priya, whom I used to prank all the time, and told her outright that I was going to join her team. I was serious about the work, and there would be no fooling around when it came to delivering results. When I told her I was prepared to start showing up in team meetings whether I was assigned to the case or not, she knew that she had no choice.

Asking for permission opens the door for denial, and in this instance I would not be denied. The willingness to aggressively go after what I wanted most had become the other personality trait that I was known for at the company, so she was aware that I would do whatever it took to get on the case. I guess stealing a steak off a partner's plate earns you that reputation.

In the months ahead, working alongside Priya to help improve the operations of an organization that I wanted to see succeed allowed me to put everything I'd learned at Bain into action. The late nights building Excel models paid off, as did all those meetings where I reluctantly took notes. I now knew how to quickly crunch numbers and present effectively in front of others. I could feel my old sense of self start to reemerge. My work wasn't perfectly aligned with my passion yet, but I now knew that when an opportunity presented itself, I would seize it without hesitation.

Mantra 8

EMBRACE THE
LIGHTNING MOMENTS

J ust as I started to settle into the rhythm of New York City living, I found out that I was nearly eligible to apply for the Bain
"externship," a six-month leave where I could work at a company
of my choice and then return to the security of my job at Bain. I
wouldn't be an official Bain employee during my leave; I would be
paid by the company that hired me for those six months, but having a safety net to return to gave me all the confidence I needed to
step out on a limb and try something new.

While most people externed at start-ups, hedge funds, or
private equity firms, some did use their time to work at nonprofits. This could be my chance to work more formally with
Scott Neeson at the Cambodian Children's Fund. In addition
to expanding its child-sponsorship program, I could use part of
my time away from Bain to backpack throughout Southeast Asia.
This was exactly the type of life I'd been dreaming about, and

I became completely focused on getting everything in order to secure my externship.

As my attention started shifting away from Bain, I started looking more deeply at my life beyond work. I was meeting some extraordinary people in New York and having more inspired conversations. My friend Dennis from SAS had put me in touch with his friend Jen Williams, who was working at a nonprofit. Dennis thought we would become fast friends, so on a Saturday morning in late September, Jen and I met for brunch. She told me about her work with the Linus Foundation, a nonprofit started by students in the Washington University class of 2006 to offer service and support to homeless youth. Over a stack of pancakes and orange juice, she explained how she managed teams across seventeen campus chapters via monthly board calls.

"How many employees do you have?" I asked.

"No, this isn't my job," she clarified. "I work in marketing at a strategic PR firm. Linus is something I do on the side."

"Oh. But what about the guys who started it? Don't they do this full-time?"

"No, this is on the side for them too. Everyone has a regular, full-time job. We do it as volunteers because we love it."

This was a revolutionary idea to me. Since I'd moved into New York City, my life had consisted of working at Bain and drinking after hours. Sometimes those two overlapped, but I'd never considered doing anything else. The concept of having any kind of extracurricular life had been buried after college. I didn't do clubs. Or take classes. Or engage in anything besides work and play.

"How can I get involved?" I asked.

*   *   *

After brunch, I met up with Dennis to walk through Central Park. It was a beautiful, warm September afternoon, the last gasp of summer; the leaves had yet to change. But a tense feeling was in the city. We were on the cusp of a total economic meltdown. Lehman Brothers had declared bankruptcy, and Bear Stearns had gone under months earlier. Layoffs were rampant. Some of my friends who had just started working were getting fired and returning home to live with their parents.

Dennis had chosen to leave his job at Bank of New York to build a start-up that allowed individuals to crowdsource funding for movie-studio films. He and Zach, the two friends I had traveled to Southeast Asia with years earlier, had successfully raised money from venture capital investors to chase their dream.

"I admire your courage to leave a secure job," I said as we meandered through the park. "But my plan is to work for the next twenty years, make as much money as possible, and then use that affluence and network to build schools throughout the developing world. But I'll only take the risk once I'm financially set." I was convinced I had it all figured out.

"You're looking at it all wrong," Dennis said. "Now is the time to take a risk. Twenty years from now you'll have a family and a mortgage. That's when you won't be able to take on risk. You'll have too much responsibility. Now is the time to take a chance, when we're young." He had a point, but he wasn't stopping there. "Besides, there's no better time to start something than when the economy is as bad as it is right now. The way I see it, at least I'm taking a shot at creating something great that will also give me executive experience—that has to be better than the guy who's about to spend twelve months on unemployment."

Dennis was right. Now was the time to take a risk.

*   *   *

That evening I was invited to the New York Philharmonic. Though I had grown up so close to New York I had never been to the symphony before.

The collective sounds of the symphony were mesmerizing, but I became even more intrigued when everyone left the stage to a rousing ovation, and an enormous man sat down alone at the grand piano. The program said that he would be playing Rachmaninoff, one of the few composers I actually knew. I wondered if just one person could stir the same emotional response from the audience that the entire symphony had just evoked.

The pianist began playing the concerto, starting with soft melodies that soon became soaring harmonies. Thunderous sounds poured from the piano. This man was crushing the keys and swaying with such force that the few hairs on his head flew from side to side. As an audience, we hung on his every note. I closed my eyes and could hear the passion he brought to his craft. I thought, *If I could feel as strongly about any one thing in the world as this man feels about his piano, I know that I would be fulfilled.*

I began to contemplate my desire to start something bigger than myself, something that could move others as well. I also thought about the revelation from Jen about creating a volunteer force and Dennis's words about taking risks while young. People think big ideas suddenly appear on their own, but they're actually the product of many small, intersecting moments and realizations that move us toward a breakthrough. I thought about the joy I'd felt while sharing those pencils across the developing world, my desire to build a school one day, and suddenly a name shot across my mind.

Pencils of Promise.

It felt as if a bolt of lightning went right through me. *Pencils* symbolized the ability to self-educate that I believed in so strongly, and *promise* had the dual meanings of making an oath or commitment to another, as well as the untapped potential we all possess. My mind surged with ideas, and my fists clenched with excitement.

At certain moments in your life you just know that everything after will change. You can ignore these moments by not acting on the new set of possibilities they enable, and your life will stay the same. But if you say yes to their reverberating potential, your life path alters permanently. This was one of those unique moments that was about to change everything. I could feel it in my bones.

I was turning twenty-five the next month, and for the past four years I had thrown my birthday-party fundraiser for the Cambodian Children's Fund. This year I could ask for $20 per person and raise $5,000, I thought. Then I could organize a holiday party to raise $4,000 to $5,000 more and eventually raise the needed funds to build a full school.

At that moment the stage at Lincoln Center went dark and the lights turned on over the audience. It was intermission.

I found my friend Ren in the aisles. "I have to go," I said.

"But it's only intermission," he replied, completely confused.

"I know, but I have to leave. Something's happened and now everything is different. I have to get to my laptop to start writing down ideas."

Ren convinced me to stay to the end of the symphony, and I sat through the second half, my mind spinning. I had planned to stop by two parties after the performance, but when I got outside Avery Fisher Hall, I texted my friends, *Not going to make it out tonight. Something big happened, I'll call you tomorrow.*

I texted my parents too: *I'm coming home tomorrow. We need to talk. I came up with an idea tonight and I need to make it happen.*

They responded, *Calm down. See you in the morning.*

Everything was coming together. I would use the externship to launch the organization, get it going during my six-month leave, then return to Bain and continue running it on the side just as Jen and her friends did theirs. I wouldn't have to leave my job to start something meaningful, nor would I have to wait a few decades to do so. Perhaps most important, after living selfishly for so long, I would build and dedicate the school to Ma. It would let her know how much she meant to me and ensure that she'd leave a legacy behind that would impact others for generations.

I rushed back to my apartment and stayed up all night writing a lengthy charter document. It began with a mission statement that included some of the following:

> Pencils of Promise intends to become a nonprofit organization with the goal of building primary education schools in areas of poverty within developing nations. Each community must display an extreme willingness to work in conjunction with the organization, as we hope to be partners in the creation of each facility. The ultimate goal for each school will be self-sustenance by the local community within five years of creation.
>
> We firmly believe that education is the single most powerful tool in the fight against poverty and disease, and that the point of greatest impact is at the primary education level where simply placing a pencil in a child's hand is the first step toward unlocking the promise of self-empowerment and a higher quality of life.

I banged out a list of possible locations for the school, potential fundraising events, and listed:

Next Steps
- Website
- Incorporate
- Speak with lawyer
- Speak with accountant
- Determine location of School 1
- Hire graphic designer to create logo
- Business cards
- Stationery/envelopes

The sun rose, and I hadn't slept at all. I took the train back to Greenwich to tell my parents about my epiphany. For years they had shot down my crazy ideas, which made me respect their opinion more than anyone else's. I knew that they were always looking out for my best interests and would give me brutal honesty. If I could win them over, the idea was a go.

After I spent twenty minutes explaining everything in detail, my mom was the first to speak: "Oh, this is crazy, but if it's for your externship, this isn't the worst idea you've had. I guess it actually kind of makes sense."

We spent the next several hours pulling the idea apart. Where would this first school be built? How would I rally funds? Who would join the initial team? The questions went on and on, but they were thorough and important. I had a lot on my plate, but the first step was clear. Someone had to put the founding deposit into a bank account.

BIG DREAMS
START WITH SMALL,
UNREASONABLE ACTS

With every conversation I had about Pencils of Promise it began to feel more real. After several weeks, it became time to file the paperwork.

While home on the first day of October, I borrowed my mom's car and drove to Town Hall. I filled out a DBA (Doing Business As) form, which allowed me to officially represent Pencils of Promise, and then drove to the local Bank of America. It was the same branch where I'd opened my first savings account.

"I'd like to open a new account," I said to the woman seated in the Small Business Services area. Her name tag read "Debbie." "It's for an organization I just started called Pencils of Promise."

"Oh, I like that name," said Debbie.

"Me too." I smiled. "What do I need to open an account?"

"Well, if you already have the yellow slip for your DBA, you need to start by making a deposit of at least twenty-five dollars."

The biggest of dreams often start with small, unreasonable acts. Most people would have thought it was crazy to start with the minimum amount, but I wanted to prove that you could start something big no matter how small you begin. And since I was turning twenty-five years old that month, I saw it as a karmic sign. I gave Debbie $25, received a deposit slip dated October 1, 2008, and walked out with a checkbook that read, "Adam Braun DBA Pencils of Promise."

I bought the domain www.pencilsofpromise.org (along with every similar sounding domain and their .com counterparts), and I went to Gmail to create a free account under the address PencilsofPromise@gmail.com. Using the new account, I emailed every friend and relative I had in the legal industry, asking if they knew someone who could help me fill out my Form 1023, the lengthy government form required to gain 501(c)(3) nonprofit status. I knew it would take months to gain nonprofit status, but the law allows you to start fundraising immediately, and once you are approved, all donations are retroactively treated as tax deductible. Fortunately, a young lawyer who worked with my uncle offered to help me complete and file all forms free of charge. We began to meet after hours, and with her help the required documents started to quickly come together.

Now with an official bank account, an email address, and the legal process under way, I began planning the first fundraiser: my annual Halloween birthday party. Every one of my mentors told me that there was no way I could raise money for a charity in such a terrible economy. But I was on a mission, armed with an ambitious dream and the practical knowledge that regardless of economic conditions, twentysomethings still went out in New York City looking for a good time. If I could throw a great party with a fun crowd that enabled people to also make a positive difference in the world, I knew that I could harvest many small contributions.

I discovered a huge space in TriBeCa, M1-5 Lounge, with a large dance floor and central bar so that people wouldn't have to wait long for drinks. I reached out to the manager about renting the space for Thursday night—the eve of Halloween. In exchange for bringing in so many people, I could charge $20 at the door, all of which would be donated to PoP. He seemed skeptical at first, but after a guarantee that I'd bring in at least two hundred people, he agreed. I had no idea if that many people would come, but I had to take a risk.

My friend Luke was working as a videographer and offered to put together an original song with a music video called "Halloween Girl" that urged people to come out to the party. Making the video was hysterical. Everyone wore absurd costumes and goofed around. But it was also moving to see how dedicated my friends were to helping raise funds for the school. I started to hear Pencils of Promise mentioned not just in my conversations, but in theirs as well. My friend Dan had always said, "Friends are the family you choose." He was right, and I couldn't have been happier with my choices.

Three weeks before the big night, I created a Facebook event invite and gave each of my friends "host" capabilities. Collectively we invited thousands of people. When we released the "Halloween Girl" video on YouTube a few days later, people began buzzing with anticipation.

I had expected a big turnout, but even I was shocked when four hundred people came. We raised $8,000—$3,000 more than I expected. The party was a blast, and throughout the event people came up to me saying, "I really want to get more involved in the organization. Let's get together sometime, I've been looking for something just like this."

*   *   *

Clearly my closest friends would help throw more parties to raise funds, but a small leadership team started to develop as well that was interested in more than just our events. My college friend Richard, a brilliant engineer who worked for one of the world's leading architects, offered to help with the design and construction of the school. My friend Libbie was working as a consultant at Deloitte, and after we pounded out ideas on napkins during our Sunday brunch, she was in too. My best friend from high school, Mike, a third-year investment banker at Goldman Sachs, asked if he could lend his skills to help manage our financials. I even recruited Jen Williams to provide expertise about running a volunteer staff. Lastly, my friend's neighbor Mimi had come to the Halloween party and told me she wanted to get more involved.

When Mimi and I grabbed drinks about a week later, she ran me through a series of ideas about how to take the organization to the next level. She wanted to be more than just a casual volunteer; she wanted to make PoP her true focus. The more we talked, the more we realized how aligned our visions were for the organization. Her energy was infectious, her work ethic was unmatched, and she produced real results. With this group, PoP had a small leadership team that began to meet in the Bain office on late nights and weekends.

As we started planning for our next major event, a holiday masquerade, I stayed up each night cold-emailing anyone I could find online who had a connection to education in Laos. I'd loved Southeast Asia most in my travels, and the two poorest countries in the region were Laos and Myanmar. Myanmar was still closed to outsiders due to political turmoil, so Laos became the obvious choice. I contacted organizations, professors, tour guides, and anyone I could find, explaining my desire to build one school and asking for their partnership, collaboration, or guidance. Much to my surprise, the first response that came in, an email from the leader of an existing nonprofit in Laos, told me to try elsewhere.

I think you have selected the wrong country to try this first endeavor. Laos has many challenges for new organizations and projects. It is not easy, he explained. When I wrote back a detailed email asking further questions, he never replied.

His words were disheartening, and the lack of a response even more so, but something inside me told me to press on. Most ventures fail in the early stages because people stop trying after they're told no too many times. Someone I reached out to for advice urged me to use my externship to work at a hedge fund rather than squander my resources at a nonprofit, but I refused to give up. At night I couldn't sleep. I stayed up until three or four in the morning searching for new leads and pursuing them.

After weeks of frantic networking attempts, an email arrived from a man named Dori, a former banker who lived in the area but fell in love with Laos and founded the organization Give Children A Choice in his retirement. He and his wife had built twenty primary schools there over the past decade. Two weeks later I found myself boarding the N train from my office in Times Square to meet them near Prince Street after work.

Over the next four hours, and several plates of french fries at the Silver Spurs café, we bonded intensely. We shared a common thread, both beginning in the business sector and finding passion through travel. Dori explained exactly how their organization worked. They asked the local community to invest 10 percent of the funding, which exemplified the same collaboration with communities that I'd come to believe in. Once or twice a year they took donors who had funded full schools to Laos, and the rest of the time their local staff member, Thongchanh, aka TC, managed the projects. With $25,000 they could build a school in three to four months; Dori even offered to send me a line-item budget.

I had already made plans to visit Laos for two weeks over my Thanksgiving break, and thanks to Dori's generosity, I now had a partner organization to show me the way, introduce me to the education ministry, and help build the first school.

Meanwhile, Mimi had found a great venue for our big masquerade party, and throughout our workdays we emailed nonstop, putting together a media kit to pitch event sponsors. I used images I had taken during my backpacking travels and refined the language from my charter document to articulate the vision and mission of the organization. When Jen encouraged me to list an audacious fundraising goal on the final page, I stated, "We seek to raise $250,000 in the next three years." At the time, that seemed incredibly ambitious.

Richard, my engineer friend who worked in architecture, joined me on my first trip to Laos over Thanksgiving. We cruised on motorbikes through the streets of Vientiane and tubed down the Nam Song River in Vang Vieng, but when rioters occupied the Bangkok airport, Richard headed back early out of fear that delays could cause him to get stuck in Southeast Asia with an expired visa. Left alone, I hopped a bus for a ten-hour trip north to Luang Prabang to meet with TC and find the village for our first school.

When I arrived at the local bus station in the mountainous region of northern Laos, it was nearly 1:00 a.m. and a starry sky sparkled above. I shared a tuk-tuk into town and found a place to crash called Rattana Guesthouse, which offered me a room with air-conditioning and a hot shower for $12.50 per night. The woman who owned it spoke English well, and the location was perfect, right in the middle of town next to the night market.

Over the next several days, TC showed me exactly why so many say that Luang Prabang is one of the most special places on earth. Colonized by the French in the late nineteenth century and named a UNESCO World Heritage Site in 1995, the charming town sits along two rivers, the Mekong and the Nam Khan. Ancient temples sit next to French colonial architecture. Saffron-robed monks walk the streets each morning at sunrise to collect alms, young children ride bicycles down bumpy streets holding pink umbrellas to shade them from the sun, and time seems to stop altogether. I immediately began to refer to it as "the land of ten thousand smiles." Never in my life had I met such peaceful, gentle people.

But beyond the idyllic landscape and wonderful people I met, the harsh reality was that most families in the countryside lived in bamboo huts with little to no education. Many lived on less than $2 per day. The poverty in the surrounding region was tremendous and overwhelming, but I had to start somewhere specific. I had to find one village in which to build the first school.

Fortunately, TC had a close relationship with many officials at the Luang Prabang Province Education Ministry and took me to meet them. They were kind and gracious, but none spoke English. When they had trouble pronouncing my first name, I decided to make it easier by simply using my initials. "Call me AB, as in *A, B, C, D*," I said. TC translated, much to their delight. They provided us with a list of the ten villages of greatest need, including such information as how many classrooms were required, which ages the school would serve, and how far it was from town.

By my final full day in Laos, we still needed to visit three more villages on the list. I wanted to see the existing school classrooms in action, meet the kids who could attend each existing school and those who could not. But it was Sunday, so no classes were in session.

Disappointed, I headed to the final village, Pha Theung, which was listed as the village with the greatest need for a preschool (which includes kindergarten) to educate children ages three to five. We passed through lush mountains and electric-green rice fields, waving to passing children along the way. When we arrived, we walked down from the dirt road to the riverside village, where we saw a three-classroom building for grades one to three with an attached bamboo hut for grade four. They didn't have anything for the younger children.

As I peeked into the bamboo room, three young girls stood unsupervised, practicing letters on the chalkboard. Not noticing me, the oldest girl whispered each word as the others wrote it out diligently. She then corrected their mistakes, urging them to work harder. She looked just like a girl I had sat next to in fourth grade. I thought of how different her life would be if she had been born elsewhere and was reminded that just a few generations ago my family lived in a small village too. As I approached to join them at the board, they immediately huddled together in embarrassment, covering their mouths to hide their laughter.

At first I wrote my name, Adam, on the chalkboard for them to see. They seemed not to understand. Remembering how I connected at the education ministry, I pointed to my chest and said in Lao, *"Khoi seu AB." My name is AB*. I wrote AB, this time in big letters, and handed the chalk to the oldest girl. By that time a small crowd of fifteen local kids had gathered inside the bamboo hut, and they giggled uncontrollably when I said, "Now you," and nodded toward the chalkboard. After much prodding, the girl quickly wrote beautiful Lao letters on the board and gave me back the chalk. "Can-tong," she said, and the kids exploded with laughter again.

After her, a different child wrote her name, then another, and then another. Alone on a Sunday, just above the river where their mothers were washing clothes and their fathers were fishing, these young children had gathered in a makeshift classroom seeking education. Although they were so excited by the sight of this strange man in their village, I think I was even more thrilled by the sight of them. I had found the place to build the first Pencils of Promise school.

The following day I flew back to New York City. We had a week to go before our masquerade fundraiser, and Mimi and the crew were finalizing logistics. We had chosen to do a party that gave everyone a chance to wear formal attire because at the time young professionals were rarely able to attend formal nonprofit events since the ticket prices were usually set too high for them to afford.

As one of the first nonprofits to exclusively advertise through Facebook and promote our event through a YouTube video, we were able to sell tickets for much less than the norm. Mimi secured liquor sponsors too, drastically reducing our costs. It worked: we sold over six hundred tickets to the event. Since our entire staff was made up of volunteers, after covering minimal costs we netted more than $20,000 that night.

By the end of the year, we had secured even more donations from people who'd learned about our approach and wanted to support us. In just three months since opening the bank account with $25, we had raised about $35,000 from more than a thousand donors. PoP didn't feel like a personal project anymore, it felt like a movement.

The difference between a lunatic and a leader is that only one of them has others who join in his or her pursuit. As much as I held the original vision of Pencils of Promise, my friends' support at that first Halloween party gave it legs. It was Mimi's pouring her heart into the masquerade, Dori and TC's introducing me to the Luang Prabang education ministry, and Richard's hopping on that flight to Laos that enabled the organization to move forward when others said it couldn't be done. Our culture glorifies founders and CEOs far too often, when in fact the early adopters and evangelists are actually the ones who make a company's success possible.

In the early days, we were a ragtag group with one common thread: belief in the impossible. We wanted to break the rules that others put in front of us and bring about a better world than the one we'd inherited. Through teamwork and dedication to a shared vision that we all collectively molded into reality, PoP was just a few months away from creating its very first school.

But just when I felt most confident, I'd failed to register that I was on the verge of getting fired from my job, and everything we'd worked so hard to create could all fall apart.

PRACTICE HUMILITY
OVER HUBRIS

I rang in the New Year basking in the glow of the uplifting experience in Laos and our fundraising successes, but it soon became clear that everything in New York was crashing around me. Companies were laying off employees in droves, the unemployed were futilely looking for jobs, and businesses were folding at an alarming rate. In this tumultuous climate, Bain called all of the third-year consultants in for a big meeting. Despite a lot of buzz about what was happening, none of us knew what to expect.

The partners sat us down in a large conference room on the twenty-fifth floor and told us they wanted to talk about potential changes in the externship. I had been counting down the days until I could get back to Laos, and I had been planning and strategizing my company-sanctioned trip with military precision. Now I worried it was all in peril.

We circled around a table with our staff manager, Rebecca. I sat biting my nails. Rebecca stared at us seriously.

"While the externship is usually six months, we are now allowing you to leave for nine months, if you'd like," she announced.

I felt flushed with relief. The policy change, Rebecca explained, helped Bain to reduce the number of people it had on the payroll without laying anyone off. Employees on externship would not receive a salary from Bain, but they would get health care and would have a job to come back to.

Maybe this wasn't fantastic news for the company, but this was fantastic news for me. I was used to living as a backpacker and subsisting on a tight budget. That skill, plus the savings I had accumulated from previous jobs, would allow me to forgo a salary while on leave. I followed Rebecca back to her office. "Where do I sign? I'm happy to go for nine months," I said.

I was in my second year at Bain and knew that if someone wasn't on an active case, they only had to come to work if they were called in. We referred to this as being "on the beach." I also knew that client work basically shut down for two weeks during Christmas and New Year's, so if you were on the beach going into that period, you basically received an extra few weeks of paid vacation. This meant that if my return date was in mid-December, I would most likely remain unstaffed until early January. I counted back nine months from that date, which landed me in mid-March. To make this work I would have to leave for my externship on March 17.

I had just a few months to prepare. It would be an absolute sprint.

To be eligible for an externship you had to be promoted to senior associate consultant (SAC), which most of my class expected to achieve. When I pitched the Bain management team my externship idea, they told me they didn't typically sanction entrepreneurial ventures. I knew that the only one who had the authority to change this was James, the New York office head. Although most of my peers were intimidated by James, I had connected with him over music. During our annual charity auction I had offered to make a monthly music mix for the highest bidder, and James bought the item. Each month I met with him to discuss his music tastes, and I'd make him a mix that both catered to his likes and introduced him to the latest tracks I had pumping through my own headphones. Our musical bond greased the wheels, and when I asked him to break precedent and let me pursue PoP during my leave, he said yes.

While the Bain leadership team agreed to let me work on PoP during my leave, the externship program still required employees to work at an existing organization. I couldn't work for PoP if it wasn't yet off the ground. Since I was committed to leaving by mid-March, I only had about five months from the moment that first bank deposit was made to get it up and running. Entrepreneurs often give up fifty-hour-per-week jobs to take on one-hundred-hour-per-week jobs, and I was trying to balance both. Although I thought I could take on absolutely anything, in time one of my two jobs started to suffer.

I decided to throw one last party before I went back to Laos in an effort to gather friends, raise more funds for the organization, and get rid of the insane amount of booze left over from the masquerade party. We'd overestimated how much we'd needed by a landslide, and I had 144 bottles of vodka sitting on the balcony of my apartment. After a friend came over and saw the sixty cases of leftover Coors Light stacked in my bedroom, he jokingly asked, "Is there something you need to tell me?"

I figured an open-bar Valentine's Day party would be a productive way to unload my stockpile. This could raise money for PoP, introduce more people to the organization, and let me reclaim some square footage in my bedroom. I found a loft for the event and set the ticket price at $40 for an all-night open bar.

At the same time, work was heating up. I was staffed on an important pitch for a postmerger integration (PMI) between two well-known banks. The project assigned me to a new manager, Prescott, who had been at Bain since he'd graduated college. He wore salmon-colored pants and was the only person I'd ever seen at the company who wrote notes on fancy, monogrammed stationery.

The project was a high-level finance pitch, and Prescott would be considered for partner if Bain could win it. As a result I was often working late, never knowing what was to come next. On the day of the Valentine's party, I was hoping to leave work at a normal hour so I could set up for the party downtown. Toward the end of the day, Prescott requested that I create a new slide, one that he referred to as our "million-dollar slide." In Bain speak, this meant it was the most important one in the presentation, the one that would win the client over. It was one slide but an enormous undertaking; the data required to make it was hidden within thousands of pages of annual reports and filings. Even if I could find the right numbers, I was worried that I didn't have the financial knowledge to create the ratios required to produce the graph needed for the slide.

I was scrambling to get the assignment done quickly, but by 8:00 p.m. I hadn't finished. All of the drinks, speakers, and party decorations were at my apartment. So were my friends Tich, Gabe, and Dan, who were helping organize everything for the 9:00 p.m. start.

My phone was blowing up.

"Where are you?" asked Tich.

150 people are coming and everything is locked at your place, texted Gabe.

I finished up feverishly, grabbing the best numbers I could find from the company reports. Just as I thought I could get out the door, Prescott called me to meet him in his office. "I need a lot more on this," he said. "You'll have to stay until midnight."

"I can't do that," I said.

"You need to finish this slide with numbers on a few more companies, and I need to see an Excel model to back up all the data used with sources cited."

I spent the next forty-five minutes riffling through reports while entering data as fast as I could. I didn't do a thorough job, but I sent it in, explained that I had an event to get to, and ran into the crowded Times Square subway station to head downtown.

I was a sweaty mess by the time I got to my apartment, but arrived in time to help Tich and Dan load the drinks into big rolling garbage cans. We packed up the speakers and supplies into a rented van and sped to the loft.

We didn't arrive until 10:00 p.m., but we still beat most of the crowd. I got a lot of *Where the hell have you been?* glances from the others who helped organize the event, but otherwise everything went off without a hitch. We sold out and raised over $10,000. It was a success. Crisis averted. Almost.

Back at work on Monday morning, I met a different fate. At 9:00 a.m. I got an email from Prescott calling me into his office.

"The data you sent me was wrong. We would have lost the case if I put this through. I stayed in the office past midnight doing the research myself to cover for your mistakes."

It was bad, but it soon got worse.

"This is some of the worst work I have ever seen. This shows me you are not capable of promotion. I can't recommend you as an SAC. I'll be recommending that you do not get promoted based on my experience with you."

I had only been working with this manager for three weeks, and he was about to ruin my career. I was furious. Whereas other managers had seen me do mistake-free work for months, this guy had only seen me at my worst. Now, everything I wanted, everything I was working so hard for, was in jeopardy.

Later that day, my staff manager, Rebecca, called me into her office. "Prescott told me that he can't recommend you get promoted to SAC, which would mean you can't go on externship. He also doesn't want you on his case anymore, so you're getting a new assignment with a new manager. You'll have five weeks to prove yourself, otherwise you won't just be out of an externship, you'll be out of a job."

She assigned me to a new internal project, an evaluation of the candidates Bain interviews and hires. They asked me to review all of the data, looking at employees' SAT scores, college grades, and how they performed once they were hired, tasking me to make correlations to find what type of person is most successful at the company. I was given a new manager, Katie, and was told, "Hopefully this thing that happened with Prescott was just a misstep. Prove to me that it was just a onetime occurrence." I had a second chance.

Fortunately, Katie and I got along great, and after slicing the data we discovered that the best consultants aren't those with a 4.0 GPA. The workplace is never perfect, so it made sense that those who were high achievers but not perfectionists could best cope with a constantly changing environment. In a matter of weeks we produced hundreds of slides for the recruiting teams. I was as stressed as I'd ever been, but when I met with Rebecca for my final review, she told me I'd been cleared for promotion and could leave on my externship.

I exhaled a huge sigh of relief. I'd learned a valuable lesson. It's in the moments when you feel most confident that you are most likely to fall flat on your face. I had taken my job at Bain for granted, assuming that I could coast into the next phase based solely on my previous accomplishments. In truth we re-create our reputation every day. Journalists with thirty years of credibility have washed their careers down the drain with one plagiarized paragraph. I had soiled months of good work with one lazy night. We each bear responsibility to prove ourselves day in and day out and have no one to blame but ourselves for the outcome. As much as I resented Prescott at the time, I later realized my three weeks with him were some of the most beneficial of my entire career. He put me in my place when it was necessary. We learn far more from our mistakes than we do from our successes, and although it nearly cost me my job and my best opportunity to start PoP, he was right to demand nothing short of excellence. I would never make the same mistakes again.

Luckily for me, the world provides us with second chances, and the timing of my promotion was perfect. The Memorandum of Understanding (MOU; the legal agreement that outlined the terms of the school's construction) for the first Pencils of Promise school was about to get signed in Laos. I needed to get to Southeast Asia fast.

Mantra 11

✳

SPEAK THE LANGUAGE OF THE PERSON YOU WANT TO BECOME

On March 17, as most of New York City was celebrating St. Patrick's Day, my Bain colleagues toasted to my last day before I headed off. Since that night at the Philharmonic, I'd spent little free time talking about my day job as a management consultant and primarily spoke with others about my aspirations for this new organization. In doing so, I spoke almost exclusively in the future tense. I tried to constantly articulate the vision for how we would create our first school, and as a result, each conversation moved things closer to reality. But I had been walking along a proverbial dock for the past five months, and now it was time to jump in headfirst. Much as when I departed for Guatemala, I didn't have much of a regimented plan beyond the first forty-eight hours. But I had faith that I could find a way to navigate the unknown territory ahead.

After an exhausting set of flights, I finally arrived in Luang

Prabang and immediately made a beeline for the familiar wooden walls of Rattana Guesthouse. We had arranged for the MOU to be signed the day after I arrived, and I desperately needed a good night's sleep. As soon as I told the owner at Rattana that I'd be staying nearly a month, she smiled politely and gave me a small but quiet bedroom with air-conditioning. "How much?" I asked.

"Ten dollars per night," she said. I was no longer in New York City, that was for sure.

The following morning, TC met me for breakfast at Joma Bakery Café, an eatery staffed by Lao locals with the best Wi-Fi and sandwiches in town. After a quick bite, I hopped on the back of TC's motorbike and we rode to the nearby education ministry office. We must have looked ridiculous, a small Lao man with a large American holding him by the waist as we pulled into a formal government ceremony. It probably didn't help that the shirt I was wearing—the only button-down I'd brought on the trip—looked like it had been stuffed in the bottom of a bag for weeks. I wasn't sure what to expect, but when we entered the room where the MOU signing would be held, I suddenly realized that this was a big deal.

Six ministry officials awaited us with a full agenda. I was told to sit at the front table with TC and the head of all preschools, while the others sat at tables facing us. A deputy introduced the attendees, who stood for a quick show of applause. No one spoke a word of English, but TC did his best to translate for me. Even though I couldn't understand the exact words, the sentiment was clear—they were deeply invested in this school's becoming a reality. I certainly understood what was expected when they handed me the official paperwork. I had reviewed the documents many times before arriving, and with a quick stroke of our pens

TC and I signed the MOU. We were officially ready to go build a school.

Three days later we were on our way to Pha Theung to attend the groundbreaking ceremony. As I bounced around the back of a gray, beat-up pickup, flanked by two men from the district education ministry, I wished so badly that just one of my friends or family could be by my side. Regardless of how much confidence I tried to project, I was twenty-five, and I still craved the comforts of camaraderie.

When we arrived, the location of the future walls had been outlined with strings, and the entire community was preparing for the big moment when we'd break ground on the build site. I couldn't believe it. I'd been speaking about this in New York for months, but to see it with my own eyes was incredible. Men, women, and young boys carried long wooden planks and gravel to the schoolyard, determined to show their dedication. When I saw two elderly grandmothers carrying a wooden plank, I rushed over to tell them that they could hurt themselves, but they smiled and shooed me away. They said something in Lao. TC told me, "They say they've been waiting their whole lives for this. You can try to stop them, but I wouldn't if I were you!" He laughed.

Eventually the children, parents, teachers, and education ministry officials all gathered for the groundbreaking ceremony. They placed a large spike in one corner, and the *nai ban* (village chief) hammered it down with force. A flurry of activity began, and within an hour the wooden planks were nailed down in place of the string outlines and the school construction was fully under way.

The education ministry had only begun to include preschools in the national education agenda within the last fifteen years, which meant that children ages three to six in most Lao villages still had no access to classrooms or teachers. Although the ministry had a strong supply of trained teachers, neither they nor the villages had the funds to build the classrooms in which children could learn.

PoP agreed to fund the construction costs for a large one-room preschool with bathrooms in Pha Theung, but only if 10 percent or more of the total project was funded by the village itself through contributions of raw materials and physical labor. This would ensure their sense of ownership, and more important, it would increase their commitment to sending their kids to the school once it opened. The education ministry agreed to provide a trained teacher and take the school under its supportive jurisdiction as well. This partnership between organizations, local government, and the village would continue to work together to support the school long term, providing school supplies, teacher salaries, and ongoing evaluations.

I recognized a few of the kids I had met in the bamboo hut several months earlier, but I was particularly ecstatic to see Can-tong, the first girl who wrote her name with me on the chalkboard. She was still incredibly shy, and if I looked in her direction, she would hide behind her giggling friends. I vowed to win her over eventually, but knew it would take time. I didn't mind; I planned to visit Pha Theung every day to help with the school construction until my Laos visa expired in a month. Then I would travel for ten weeks through several other countries in Southeast Asia, until returning to Laos at the start of July to see the school construction completed.

We spent the rest of the afternoon eating delicious fish caught from the river, playing games with the excited children, and witnessing the school come to life. I had pictured this day for months, but it was far more powerful than anything I could have anticipated. I thought of my grandfathers, who had journeyed across foreign lands, just as I was doing now. I thought of my grandmothers, who had dedicated so much of themselves to their children and grandchildren, just as the women carrying those planks had as well.

As we drove back to town, I pulled on my sunglasses and looked out the window, hoping the others in the car wouldn't notice the tears streaming down my face. This school, my dream, was happening right in front of me.

The next two weeks were busy with getting the school off the ground—literally. Each morning at the guesthouse, a Lao woman in her late twenties, Lanoy, would offer me breakfast with a cheery smile. Her job was to do the laundry and change the bedsheets, but she had learned from the guesthouse owners to speak perfect English, and she had enough moxie to practice with the travelers that passed through. After chatting with her about my day's plans, I'd ride my motorbike an hour to Pha Theung to play with the kids and check in on the school's progress, twisting through valleys and over bridges, blasting the Rolling Stones and the Raconteurs the whole way.

I spent the mornings digging ditches, carrying bricks, and laying cement with the laborers, and the afternoons playing games and swimming in the river with the children. The routine became so normal that as soon as the children finished lunch and received their afternoon break, they would grab my hand to run down the hill behind the schoolyard, squealing with delight and pushing their siblings into the warm, shallow waters. Some days I'd race a group of ten-year-old boys out to a large rock jutting from the river, and on other afternoons they would take me fishing using handmade nets in an old wooden canoe.

As I floated in the river I often wondered, *What are my friends doing at this very moment?* They were at swanky parties or sitting in important meetings with important people, and I was in the mountains swimming and playing Duck, Duck, Goose. I couldn't have been happier with my choice. It was the simplest life I'd ever known, and the most fulfilling too.

One afternoon, while waiting for some older kids to get out of class in their makeshift school, I sat under a tree writing in my journal. When I heard soft voices murmuring over my shoulder, I turned around to the sight of three young girls. They were covered in dirt and wearing tattered clothes, with no one looking after them at all. For some reason I decided to record a quick video, so I turned on my camera and asked them, *"Jao seu nyang?" What's your name?*

"Nuth," replied the first one, sinking her face behind folded hands. When I asked the other two for their names, Nuth instinctively perked up and answered on their behalf. Her two adorable friends, Tamund and Nith, stood beside her eagerly smiling. I then panned the camera around the schoolyard, showing the three-room primary school, the bamboo hut, and the site where our first school—a preschool for children ages three to five—was under way. As I swung the camera back toward them, I was struck by a sudden realization.

"And you're going to be our first preschool students?" I asked. Once again, I figured the first step toward this becoming a reality was to verbalize it aloud. Although they didn't know a word of English, all three giggled with a sense of understanding. "Sounds good?" I asked, and they laughed again with delight. The moment perfectly captured the beauty and innocence of these young girls that our school would educate. It also demonstrated the interconnectedness that we all share as a global humanity, regardless of whether we look the same or speak the same language.

That night I posted the clip on Facebook, tagging every person who had worked so hard to contribute toward that first school. I was determined to make PoP as transparent as possible by showing people that their donations, regardless of size, were going to change lives in a profound way.

When I woke up the next morning, I saw that the response to the video was overwhelming. Overnight I had received emails, messages, and comments from friends and strangers alike. All of them wanted to get involved. The school was no longer just about my personal desire to thank Ma for her sacrifices. It was now about these three little girls and the countless others we could impact if we started a broader movement.

A friend soon connected me by email to Bob Anderson, the founder of Community Learning International, an organization that built community learning centers, libraries, and schools in Luang Prabang Province. We met for dinner one night along the banks of the Mekong, and Bob explained that he had been living in Laos for more than a decade. His knowledge of the country, people, and NGO space was impressive.

"How much do you pay for a classroom?" asked Bob.

"We work in partnership with the education ministry and a partner organization, so they provide us with a detailed budget, and then we pay them to hire the contractor," I said. "The school under construction is one large room and a bathroom, and after the village contributes more than ten percent of the cost, we pay about fifteen thousand dollars."

"We build school classrooms for ten thousand dollars."

I couldn't believe it. How were they able to do it for $5,000 less?

Bob explained that his organization had a local architect on staff, Somlath, and that after they received government approval for all of their builds, money never left their organization except to pay salaries and buy building materials directly from the wholesalers at local prices. They bypassed contracting companies by doing all the work themselves. I didn't even know that was possible.

When Bob offered to have his architect, Somlath, take me to visit several villages they were scouting for potential sites, I jumped on the opportunity. "I want you to see Phayong village in particular," Bob said. "We've wanted to work there for years but currently lack the funds."

Days later I was bouncing around the back of a tuk-tuk with Somlath, headed four hours north to Phayong. He explained that during the rainy season from June to September, mudslides washed away the dirt road that careened around the hairpin mountainside, making Phayong completely inaccessible to the outside world. At several points on our nail-biting journey toward the village, we had to hop out of the tuk-tuk to push it up a hill. We pushed with all of our strength, hoping our extra force would will the vehicle onward and not leave us stranded in the wilderness. Thankfully, it worked and we arrived just before sunset.

The entire village was made up of bamboo huts with no electricity. Children roamed naked, and mothers carried babies in slings on their backs. Half of Phayong's more than five hundred inhabitants were ethnic Hmong and the other half were Khmu. Although they lived and farmed side by side, they could not communicate because they spoke different languages. The only chance for a unified future was through education. At the center of the village stood a small one-room structure with decaying wooden bars and a rusted corrugated-tin roof.

"They use this as their school," Somlath said.

"For which grade?" I asked.

"All grades. This is all they have, so they only teach children from ages ten to twelve. They have been requesting a school for fourteen years here."

As I shook my head in disbelief, a young boy walked past us. Somlath began chatting with him in the local dialect, then turned back to me. "He is eight years old. The younger children can't go to school here because they have no classrooms or teachers, so he cannot read or write his own name."

"Ask him, if he could have anything in the world, what would he want?"

Somlath listened and translated, "He would like to go to school, Mr. AB."

Sometimes you know something in your head, and other times you know it in your heart. The mind delivers logic and reason, but the heart is where faith resides. In moments of uncertainty, when you must choose between two paths, allowing yourself to be overcome by either the fear of failure or the dimly lit light of possibility, immerse yourself in the life you would be most proud to live.

I had had no idea what would happen when I'd arrived in Laos that month. I hadn't known whether the MOU ceremony would be successful, whether we would truly break ground on our first school, or if I could share any of it with our supporters back home. But I had faith that it would work out, and that faith gave me the confidence to speak the language of the person I wanted to one day become. The more we speak in the voice of our most aspirational self, the closer we pull our future into our present. That's what compelled me to put $25 into a bank account, brought Nuth, Nith, and Tamund into my life, and carried me on a broken-down tuk-tuk across towering mountains into a village that desperately needed a school for its most vulnerable young people.

We stayed in a shabby bamboo hut in Phayong that night, resting on hard mats, listening to dogs bark at the shimmering moon. Since arriving in Laos, I'd slept pretty well, but that night I was wide-awake. I was already envisioning the second Pencils of Promise school.

WALK WITH A PURPOSE

After nearly a month, the foundation was laid on our first school and my visa was approaching expiration, so I left to explore the surrounding countries for several months before returning to see the school's completion. They say, "Not all who wander are lost," and my travels now took on a distinct purpose. I was eager to learn from locals and NGOs in the surrounding areas. I started in a remote part of southern Laos referred to as the Four Thousand Islands. On the island of Don Det, a Frenchman who worked for a health-based organization invited me on an adventure to a remote village one afternoon. He would be accompanying an elderly Lao woman, who was returning to her home after being away for more than forty years.

We spent the following day hiking eight hours across rice fields that few eyes had ever seen. When we arrived, we were greeted at the village with local delicacies, such as duck-blood soup and rice whiskey, and plenty of Lao dancing, but the journey there was even more memorable. We drank delicious freshwater straight from a river, marveled at the brightest rainbow I'd ever seen, and learned that when one family in a village decides to build a new home, the community as a collective participates in the project. That one conversation triggered the idea for what would become PoP's Promise Committees, cohorts of four mothers and four fathers that we organized to oversee the development of each school we built.

After a week in the Four Thousand Islands, I met up with a friend and traveled south. We visited the floating village of Brunei (the largest in the world), where we noticed tiny boats filled with young children in matching white uniforms. A mother standing along the dock pointed to one of the vessels and explained, "School bus!" Seeing that, I realized that finding safe transportation is something many parents must consider when deciding whether to send their child to school; this consideration would factor in when PoP later launched scholarship programs. In addition to providing a backpack, uniform, school supplies, and exam fees, we decided to cover the cost of safe transportation as well.

In Bali, I visited David Booth, a brilliant British civil engineer who founded an NGO called the East Bali Poverty Project. He shared a series of documents outlining his entire methodology and approach, and I spent time with his team studying their education, nutrition, and agricultural programs. I was incredibly impressed by David's ability to train a team of men and women from Indonesia to lead all operations. Many Western organizations never transition leadership into local hands, which in my eyes demonstrated a lack of commitment to long-term sustainability. After spending time with David, I vowed to find my first local staff member when I returned to Laos.

On my last morning in Bali, I awoke with my shirt drenched in a cold sweat. Excruciating pain racked my entire body. Something was very, very wrong. Was it dehydration, dengue fever, or something else? I had no time to find out because I had to fly to Bangkok in three hours to make a connecting flight to Kathmandu, where I would meet my dad, who was flying in for two weeks of hiking in Nepal. Apart from my work in Laos, trekking the Himalayas with my dad was going to be the highlight of my four-month-long trip. We had talked about it for years, and there was no way I could miss it.

Delirious, I took a taxi to the airport, and after arriving in Bangkok, I had to walk through the thermal-image scanner that was set up at customs to detect anyone who had an elevated temperature. I set off the machine right away. Two men from airport security escorted me to a quarantined area where they took my temperature. I had a fever of 103.4 degrees Fahrenheit. They immediately placed a Michael Jackson–style mask over my mouth and told me that I would be placed in the hospital for a week of tests. *I can't spend the next week in a Thai hospital,* I thought. I had to make my connecting flight to meet my dad.

"I'm fine, just a small headache," I said. "Nothing is wrong."

"No, something is wrong," said a Thai security officer with a stern face.

"I need to leave."

"No, you need to go to the hospital. Go to the nurse waiting for you in the corner."

Joel Puac had once instructed me to always walk with a purpose. If you look like you know what you are doing, people will assume the same. I walked straight up to the nurse, looked her in the eyes, and said confidently, "You're supposed to sign this form so I can leave." She looked around for secondary approval, but no one was nearby. I kept my eyes fixed directly on hers, hoping that my poker face wouldn't give away the biggest bluff I'd ever tried to pull off.

It worked: she signed the form and I quickly slipped out without anyone's noticing. I bolted through immigration, grabbed my bag, and jetted out of the airport toward the Silver Gold Garden, a cheap hotel nearby, in hopes that a night's rest would kick-start a recovery. Shivering and with a cold towel on my head, I emailed my dad, *I'll need to see a doctor as soon as I land, but I'll see you at the airport in Nepal.*

After I arrived in Kathmandu, I was bedridden for several days. Eventually my fever broke, and I managed to do about half the trek, but I felt awful the entire time. Fortunately, my dad tended to me as never before, barely leaving my bedside. I guess those with hard exteriors sometimes have the softest interiors.

After our two weeks together, he headed back to the States, and I met with Agatha Thapa, who in the 1970s founded the organization Seto Gurans, which now delivers early-childhood-education programs in villages across fifty-nine of Nepal's seventy-five districts. Her programs enable women to use items they can find in their rural villages—fruits, vegetables, string, tire scraps—to create a curriculum for teaching young children. This relationship would be pivotal: a year later Agatha took in our first PoP Fellow, who lived in Nepal for four months observing her holistic education model, which helped lay the foundation for our programs to teach transferable skills within each community where we build a school.

On my last day in Nepal, protests against the government swept across the entire city of Kathmandu. All transportation, banks, and businesses were shut down. Since no taxis were in operation,

I found a Nepali man peddling a bicycle-operated tuk-tuk who agreed to ride forty-five minutes across the city to get me to the airport. After I paid his fee up front, we took off.

As we got closer to the city's main intersection, I heard loud chants coming closer and closer. The streets were filled with people shouting with rage. When we tried to cross the intersection, hundreds of men carrying sticks suddenly converged on us from all sides. They surrounded the tuk-tuk, screaming angrily, shaking their sticks and clubs in my direction. My heart raced with fear. A scene from the book *Shantaram*, which I'd recently read, in which angry mobs beat and dismember people in seconds, played in my head. The tuk-tuk driver turned to me and with panic in his voice said, "Get out."

Before I could protest, he said, "You have to get out right now."

As I stepped down to the ground, I was surrounded on all sides by an enraged crowd. I did the only thing I could think of: I clasped my hands together and repeated the phrase of respect in Nepal and India, *namaste* (meaning, "I bow to you" or "the light in me honors the light in you"), over and over. I tried to explain to anyone who would listen that I was only trying to get to the airport.

As the furious mob surged, the tuk-tuk driver started talking with the ringleader. After they finished, the driver turned and said, "You will walk the rest of the way. Take your bag, they will not let you ride anymore, and leave quickly."

Without hesitation I threw on my backpack and walked through the crowd. *Walk with a purpose*, I told myself. Feigning confidence, I looked straight ahead as if I knew where I was going and followed wherever my legs would take me. When I finally left the swarming intersection unscathed, I let out a sigh of relief, asked a kind woman for directions, and walked several miles on foot to the airport's barricaded entrance.

My heart was still pounding, but I felt terrible for not thanking the tuk-tuk driver. His willingness to stand up for a complete stranger had saved me from a potentially fatal beating. He risked his own safety, not for any reward, but because it was the right thing to do.

In any confrontation, most people focus on the perpetrator and the victim. There is an inherent expectation that had one of these two acted differently, the outcomes of a conflict may have been averted. But the greatest opportunity actually exists within the role of the bystander, the person who neither benefits nor gains from the event itself. When a bystander steps up on behalf of a potential victim, just as that tuk-tuk driver did for me that day on the streets of Kathmandu, he or she becomes the very definition of a hero. We are more often bystanders to conflict than we are victims or perpetrators, and with that comes the recognition that we have a moral obligation to defend others, even when the crosshairs of injustice aren't pointed at us personally.

When I returned to Luang Prabang, as usual I headed to Rattana Guesthouse, but this time I asked to meet with the young woman Lanoy, who changed the bedsheets and greeted the guests. Since meeting David Booth in Bali, I had been thinking about finding a Lao local to coordinate the builds in-country. Lanoy kept coming to mind. She possessed an incredible work ethic and seemed eager to take on more than her role at the guesthouse asked of her.

When I had the chance to sit down with her, she told me about how on weekends she volunteered to bring food to families in the countryside, and that she dreamed of one day helping the children of her country. I shared my vision for Pencils of Promise, where trusted local staff would lead all local operations. I then asked her to become our first local coordinator, explaining that we didn't have any money for salaries at the outset, but I would invest in training her.

I promised to coach her on public speaking, sending her first email, managing a team, and most important, commanding the respect of men and women in every room she entered. "I would like this very much," she responded, "but first you have to ask my mom for permission."

That night I put on my button-down shirt, tucked it into my jeans, and asked Lanoy's surrogate mother (the woman who ran the guesthouse and had taken in Lanoy years earlier) for permission to bring her on as our volunteer coordinator. She agreed on a trial basis, but said Lanoy could join me only after she had completed her weekly work at the guesthouse. We were both ecstatic.

Three days later I invited Lanoy to join me on a trip to visit potential sites for future schools and see our nearly completed one in Pha Theung. I asked her to bring a pad and pen so that she could speak with locals and record data on each prospective community. She nodded her head in solemn agreement and met with me early the next morning for breakfast at Joma.

As we sat down with the chief of Kok Niew, the first village we visited that day, Lanoy proudly pulled out her new notebook. The inside contained neatly lined graph paper, but my jaw dropped when I saw that on the cover of her notebook was a cartoon picture of the grinning shark from *Finding Nemo*. This would never have been allowed at Bain, but I wasn't at Bain anymore. I was in the mountains of Laos, where Lanoy's "Shark Book" would one day hold the contents that would lead her to educate thousands.

The long day ended with a visit to Pha Theung, where the school's construction was in its final stages. The energy in the schoolyard was palpable. I returned several times over the next week, each day taking photos of the progress to share with our supporters back home.

On my final afternoon, I returned to my roots by passing out pens and pencils. Nith, Nuth, and Tamund accepted theirs gladly, and Can-tong finally emerged from behind a group of friends to take hers as well. At first she was extremely timid, but once she held that pencil in her hand, I could see her begin to transform. As I walked up to the road to take my motorbike back to town, the last thing I saw was Can-tong skipping away, singing loudly. She was headed somewhere fast, and she was moving with purpose.

HAPPINESS IS FOUND
IN CELEBRATING OTHERS

My four months in Southeast Asia had come to an end, but the next leg of the journey was about to begin back home. On Ma's eightieth birthday my family planned a big dinner in New York City. The night before, I asked her if we could spend some time alone.

"I want to share something with you," I said.

She was curious. Although she was my grandmother, and we were close, I rarely asked to see her alone for private chats. Ma knew that I'd started PoP and had been traveling back and forth to Laos. She was aware that I had taken a sabbatical from Bain, but figured I was just the traveling type in my twenties. Like all Jewish grandmothers, she was prone to worry and was completely opposed to my doing anything that required travel far away from her.

She would tell me, "Why do this, go to these places where people have so little, when you have such nice things here? Trust me, I know! I lived like one of them, so why don't you stay here close to your family and be happy with the nice things you have?"

While I understood where she was coming from, I also understood that she didn't know what motivated me. On this night, I would make it clear.

"What is it you want to share with me?" she asked, bobbling as she walked toward me.

I sat Ma down. She's small, five feet three, and was wearing all beige. She always wears matching clothes, all purple, all beige, a monochromatic uniform. And she always says she doesn't look good, but she does. She grabbed my hand with both of hers and started petting me.

"I want to show you what I have been doing," I said. "I want you to know why I went to build a school."

I took out what I prepared—three pictures. The first was of Nith, Nuth, and Tamund. I explained the story of how I met them one day while the school was under construction, and how excited they were to attend their first classes. I told Ma about how this school would radically change their lives.

"Oh, this is amazing." She nodded, beginning to grasp some of what I felt.

The second picture was of the completed school in Pha Theung. Its white walls shone brightly against its red roof and blue shutters. "Oh, this is so much. So beautiful. You know something, this looks just like the school I went to! Before they made me stop going to school and sent me to the camps, this is what my school looked like," she said in her Hungarian accent.

"Now I want to show you what motivated me. This picture is the reason that I went to all of those foreign places, traveled to all of these communities, and took a break from my job. This is what

I wanted to create most in the world." I showed her the third picture, which was of the large sign above the entrance to the school.

She squinted to read the sign, but couldn't without her glasses. "Wait one second, I get my glasses." She pointed her finger on each word as she slowly whispered them aloud.

"'Luang Prabang Education Department, Give Children a Choice, Pencils of Promise. 2009.'" She paused, looked over at me, and smiled. She then looked back and continued, "'Lovingly dedicated to . . .'"

She covered her mouth with her hands as her jaw opened. Her hands began to tremble. She looked over at me and her eyes welled with tears. She looked back at the picture and continued reading, "'Lovingly dedicated to Eva Braun. . . .'" She burst into tears, and so did I. We tried to speak, but neither of us could talk. She just reached over and squeezed my hand. We sat side by side and cried tears of joy.

"This is so much. Why, why for me?" she asked.

"You did so much for me, Ma. You have been through so much. I couldn't get you golf clubs or some gift certificate. I wanted to do the most meaningful thing I could for you, so that you would know that your legacy would last, and your survival will make the lives of others better. I started Pencils of Promise so that I could build a school and dedicate it to you."

We cried and hugged, and after composing ourselves, Ma replied, "Adam, I wish I knew the words to describe this feeling. It feels like this is why I survived. I survived for this. It feels like it's all coming back to me, everything I suffered for is coming back to me, but in good ways. All the bad things I went through were for these good things to happen."

I nodded, still unable to speak, digesting the weight of what she had just said. We exist because of the sacrifices of those who came before us, but how often can we make them feel the full value of their impact?

Through this one school, I was now connected more deeply to my grandmother than ever before. It was only by focusing on creating joy in her life that I discovered the greatest feelings of happiness in my own. I knew that we could enable this same experience of building and dedicating a school for so many others, and in doing so we would give them the chance to honor the people they loved most. The vibrancy that PoP instilled in my daily life was contagious, and I could see it now flickering in Lanoy and Mimi and so many others. We now had to figure out how to get that flame to spread.

FIND THE IMPOSSIBLE ONES

W hile I had been traveling throughout Southeast Asia, coordinating the construction of our first school and building the organization on the ground, PoP continued to evolve on the other side of the world in New York. Mimi led our first white party—where everyone wore their finest white attire—which attracted eight hundred people, our largest event yet. As always, all of the party proceeds went toward school projects. Every single contribution, regardless of its size, was tremendously valuable.

Armed with more knowledge of project costs, we demonstrated the impact of each ticket: $30 could buy fifteen books, $40 could buy bookshelves, $60 purchased teacher supplies. People loved that they were able to see the correlation and impact. The event sold out three days in advance, and afterward my inbox was once again flooded with messages from people interested in getting more involved.

Although I didn't drink coffee, I offered to "grab coffee" with anyone who wanted to join our volunteer force. One of my founding beliefs was that even if people didn't have money to donate, which few twentysomethings during the financial crisis did, they could still add value through other forms of donation. Their time, energy, and skills could help us advance our mission. Every conversation began with the same question: "What do you love doing most?" Once I understood that person's passion, we could craft a way for him or her to use it to support PoP. Through that approach, our volunteer force expanded rapidly.

At the same time, I was focused on finding a way to make the organization sustainable for the long haul. I called George Stanton, my mentor who had first encouraged me to choose Bain over Lehman, and asked for his advice. His answer was direct: "Listen, Adam, you need to find five pillar donors who will give you fifty thousand dollars each. This way you'll have a quarter million dollars to start, and from there you can figure things out."

His advice surprised me because it was so far from what I'd planned on doing. We had seen that many small acts add up to make a large difference. Ninety-eight percent of our unique donations had been in amounts of $100 or less from people in their teens and twenties. These small donors funded our first school entirely and had put the funds in the bank for several more. I wanted to stay true to this approach until we had a proven track record that would merit our asking for major contributions.

George told me I was crazy. "In this financial environment, that'll be impossible."

His words stung. It's hard to hear anyone say that something you believe in isn't possible. But this burned even more because it came from someone whose opinion I valued so much. It also propelled me forward. It forced me to think more deeply about our fundraising approach and helped me define the type of person that we would need to recruit. I needed to find staff and donors who would get excited about doing something others deemed impossible.

For us to be successful, we had to bet on two early hypotheses. If correct, we would be incredibly well positioned to grow in the years ahead, and to help change the landscape for how a modern organization was built. If I was wrong, we would most likely fold within twenty-four months.

The first big bet was on the rise of social media. Mark Zuckerberg founded Facebook as a sophomore in the class of 2006 at Harvard while I was a sophomore at Brown (one of the first ten schools to use the platform). Unlike our parents, we didn't view social media as foreign; it was woven into the fabric of our everyday lives. It didn't take a genius to see that social media would one day penetrate almost every facet of popular culture. But few people in the nonprofit world understood this yet because social media was still viewed as the space for college and high school kids. Most people were only focused on courting their major donors. But I didn't just want donors, I wanted outspoken advocates. I genuinely believed that someone's Facebook status was a valuable commodity. Viewing an individual's social media presence as an important form of currency was something we banked on early.

The second big bet was on the rise of cause marketing. All data suggested that consumers would overwhelmingly choose a product that makes the world better if compared to an equal product that didn't have an element of social good. As a result, I believed that marketers and major brands with lots of advertising dollars would want to keep those consumers happy by finding ways to show them how their purchases benefited others. I figured they would seek out as partners the organizations with the largest and most engaged social media followings. So we focused on building an engaged community online and transparent programs that created tangible good on the ground, making us a perfect fit for cause-marketing campaigns.

If the world moved in the direction we believed it would, we would be well positioned to springboard forward in the years ahead. But we couldn't capitalize on either area without top-notch branding and design.

Because of this, I became obsessed with building "the brand" of Pencils of Promise. I considered everything from the colors and shape of our logo, to the language we used in our print materials, to the imagery and architecture of our website. Branding can make or break a company, and a great brand creates legitimacy and trust, both of which are essential in the nonprofit world. While I could envision our brand in my head, I had absolutely no design skills. Some nights I would open Photoshop or InDesign, but within an hour I'd grow frustrated. If Mimi was the organization's right hand, I desperately needed a left hand that could design the shit out of things.

Fortunately, I received a random email from a guy I'd grown up with but hadn't spoken to in almost ten years. Brad Haugen was working at a leading advertising agency and wanted to use his talents for good. He had been following our progress through social media and was confident that he could leverage the marketing and design expertise of his company, Bartle Bogle Hegarty (BBH), to help us build a world-class brand. A few weeks later, a friend from SAS connected me with a rising star in the commercial photography world, Nick Onken. After a lengthy lunch together, he agreed to fly himself to Laos to shoot stunning photography on our behalf. Suddenly, I had a branding dream team coming together.

Brad began recruiting a volunteer team that expanded to include technologists, advertisers, bloggers, and designers. Now that we had people all over the city working on the organization, I borrowed a page from Scott Neeson's playbook and had fifty sets of business cards made for $2.50 per set through a Vistaprint.com promotion. All volunteers who took an active role in the organization received their own business card, listing their name and a title I made up. I usually mailed the cards to these people without even telling them they were coming, but the feedback was always the same: "I'm handing out my PoP card twice as much as my actual business card!" It became a part of their nightly conversations, and it soon became a meaningful part of their lives.

I wasn't just interested in building one school anymore. I wanted to build a movement that changed people's perception of charity. And although I didn't have deep pockets behind me at the start, I had a far more potent weapon—conviction in a set of unique beliefs. When you align individually high-performing people around the idea that they are collectively underdogs, you tap into the cohesive gel that brings early adopters together. We created an enemy for us to rebel against (this belief that our approach was "impossible"), which is one of the fastest ways to unite people around a common goal. And with each new person who joined our volunteer army, we received both the validation and the skills necessary to prove that we could carve a different path from those who came before us.

But we had to find and inspire new torchbearers to carry these ideas forward beyond New York City. We had to find people who would test the edge of the world by feeling its curves. It was time to take PoP on a road trip across the entire country.

Mantra 15

— ✳️ —

FOCUS ON ONE PERSON
IN EVERY ROOM

After months of toying with the idea, my four best friends and I agreed to fly to Los Angeles, rent a thirty-five-foot RV, and drive across the country to spread the word about Pencils of Promise.

My friend Gabe, after working in consulting for several years, was able to persuade the firm he worked at to allow him to take a brief sabbatical. Tich was in the midst of starting a small business. Dan was a guitarist launching a band that could book gigs in various cities along the way, and Luke wanted to hone his documentarian skills by shooting footage across the nation. We figured that the PoP message would resonate with a younger audience, especially because we were so young ourselves, so we laid out an itinerary of college campuses to visit.

The first stop on the college tour was Oklahoma State University, a school with thirty-five thousand students and the alma mater of my SAS roommate, Jaret. Dan had contacted the school to set up the speech through its student affairs department, so we anticipated hundreds of students in a massive auditorium. Luke brought his camera and sound equipment, calibrating everything the night before so we could capture the cheering throngs of students perfectly. I even got a Facebook message the day before the speech from a sophomore student, Chelsea Canada, asking us to save her a seat because she might be a bit late.

The night before, I could barely sleep. I was going to give my first major speech. I was nervous and excited to bring my message to a college campus. In the minutes before the scheduled start time, I paced in the bathroom, practicing lines in my head.

I was so focused on my speech, I didn't give any thought to what I would do if no one showed up. But the room never filled up. I gave it an extra twenty minutes for the students to come, but they never did. I went to the podium in front of five people—my four best friends, and one OSU student. Chelsea Canada.

It was a far cry from what I expected, and it was hard not to feel embarrassed about the thirty-slide presentation I'd prepared, which I was now essentially delivering to an audience of one. But it wasn't a lost opportunity. One person was there, and I knew well that it only takes one person to make a huge difference. Not wanting to disappoint, I gave as passionate a speech as I could for the next forty-five minutes. I could tell that the message struck a chord with Chelsea, and afterward I assured her that if she made this organization her passion, something magical would happen.

It wasn't the speech I planned on giving, but it made an immediate impact. We had occasional Internet access on our computers in the RV, and by the time we returned from a late lunch, Chelsea had added me on Facebook. When I clicked into her full profile, I saw the entire thing was about PoP. Her profile pic was now our logo, she'd started a "PoP at Oklahoma State University" group, and she'd posted a status update linking to a ninety-nine-second animated video that Brad and his BBH colleagues had made about the organization.

She launched our first PoP club on her campus and a few months later presented at her old high school about us. She passed that infectious passion on to another young student, Andrew Gray, who launched our organization in his high school—and opened the door for us to work on the high school level across the country. He eventually spearheaded the creation of PoP high school clubs across the entire country, became president of the PoP Club at Oklahoma State University after Chelsea, and gave a TEDx Talk about his involvement in the organization. To top it off, his work was profiled in multiple press features, celebrating him, and further extending the reach of our message.

PoP operated, in part, through the ripple effect. We knew one individual's commitment could spread to his or her family, friends, and peers, becoming a part of the value system they passed down to future generations. With this idea, our mission grew from building schools throughout the developing world to also training young leaders to take action at home and abroad. This led to our early PoP slogan, "A generation empowered will empower the world."

We saw this play out again and again as we traveled to college campuses across the country. We went to the University of Texas, where Tich knew the captain of the cheerleading team. This would be my second speech, and we expected a much bigger turnout given his connection.

Wrong again. Eight people came. But one of them was a student named Alex, who moved to New York City that summer to become our first official intern. She, like Andrew Gray, later attended Semester at Sea, both of them wanting to explore the vast world beyond their own backyard.

In Alabama we met a hysterical elderly woman running a restaurant who gave us our favorite line of the trip. "Honey, a stranger's just a friend I haven't met yet!" she proclaimed. It was hokey, but it was true, and we experienced it again and again on the road.

When I gave a speech at Tulane, the room was finally packed, this time with about fifty students who were studying international development. One student met up with us for a beer later that night and in the months ahead began organizing concerts to benefit PoP.

I started to realize that it didn't matter how many people were in the room. If I could inspire just one person to take one action on our behalf (organize an event, donate his or her birthday, or launch a PoP club), then the organization would have a committed individual to carry it forward. In Chelsea and Andrew and Alex I had seen the impact of having an anchor.

So with every speech I gave, whether to a large or a small audience, I focused on finding the one person whose eyes lit up most when he or she heard our story for the first time. It took lots of practice to identify that person during a talk, and I still work on it with every speech I give, but the goal is always the same—find one person in every room and convert him or her into the next Chelsea Canada.

After three weeks on the road, late October arrived, and we flew back from Atlanta to New York for twenty-four hours to throw my annual Halloween birthday fundraiser. It had been one year since we started. In 365 days we had pursued an impossible idea, built a school, and sparked a small movement. It was time to celebrate the organization's accomplishments and also raise some money.

To liven things up, I bought five bumblebee costumes and

insisted we wear them through airport security. We rocked antennae and wings and tight black shorts over black stockings, and people couldn't help but crack up. The five burly bumblebees brought some serious Halloween spirit onto that Delta flight to JFK. We carried it into the party that night, greeting every one of the guests that showed up, raising another $10,000 from small but meaningful contributions.

Time was running out before my externship ended, so I planned two last trips, one to Nicaragua and another to Laos. I kept hearing people refer to PoP as "that Laos organization" when the goal was to become an organization working with children globally. I decided that we should establish a presence in each of the three major poverty zones—Asia, Latin America, and Africa—so that we could ensure our work was replicable on a global scale. Latin America would be next. I found a partner organization called Seeds of Learning that worked in Nicaragua, and after many phone calls and emails, I spent two weeks in the country to lay the foundation for a partnership.

Months earlier I'd received a Facebook message from Leslie Engle, whose best friend had attended SAS with me and shared my contact information after seeing the pictures I was posting on Facebook. Leslie wrote that she was moving to Luang Prabang toward the end of the year. She had backpacked there years earlier, and with her background as a writer and preschool educator, she planned to work in Laos for several years and find a happier way of life. After exchanging a few messages, we arranged an hour-long phone call that went amazingly well. She was different from our New York City volunteers. She'd traveled extensively through the developing world and had a strong grasp of how to live and work with rural communities. She also knew how to educate. She was an "on the ground" person through and through, but I wasn't ready to take on a full staff in Laos. I was still covering all travel and administrative costs out of my own pocket, so that every dollar raised went into our schools. "Hopefully we'll link up when we both head there in December," I said to clarify how little I could commit.

After returning from Nicaragua, I emailed her a few days before my marathon flights to Laos and found out we were both arriving the same morning. We had separately booked the same flight into Luang Prabang, which is where we met for the first time. The serendipity of it all was too strong to ignore. The next afternoon Nick Onken showed up to shoot photographs, and for six straight days the three of us rode motorbikes across the Laos countryside. We made a great travel trio, and some days Lanoy was able to finish early at the guesthouse and join us as well.

Just days before I headed back to New York City, we went up north to the village of Phayong for the opening ceremony of our second school. Lanoy translated the ceremony for us while taking notes in her Shark Book, except at one point when she interrupted a speech by one of the many men sitting around us. Everyone in the room seemed to be shocked.

The ceremony then progressed, but we had no idea what'd happened. Later, she explained, "That man was saying how happy he was about the school, but he started asking for more things. I told him that Pencils of Promise does not give handouts. The village needs to prove that they will use this school well. It's up to us as Lao people, not you and Leslie and Nick, to prove we are dedicated to the education of our children." In that part of the world, women rarely interrupted men the way Lanoy had. I knew in that moment that she was exactly the person I wanted in charge of our local programs. She was our anchor. The petite woman I first encountered doing laundry at the guesthouse was turning into a bold, confident leader.

With two completed schools, a plan for expansion into other regions, and a solid group of supporters, we'd come much further than I could ever have expected in my nine-month externship.

Leslie had only known me for a week, but she kept asking me the same question: "How will you go back to being a consultant?"

"It's not going to be a problem at all," I assured her. I genuinely believed every word I said. I thought I'd be fine. I had never been so wrong about anything in my entire life.

Nuth on the steps of the first Pencils of Promise school.
(Photograph by Nick Onken)

Ready to see
photos, videos, and more?

GO TO THE WEBSITE
www.AdamBraun.com/Book

You'll find

- Photos from beautiful locations
- Videos of the book's main characters
- Icons to download for each mantra

READ THE SIGNS
ALONG THE PATH

After your third year at Bain's New York office, nearly every member of the class is expected to either go on to business school and then return to the company, or avoid business school and go to work elsewhere. Recruiters knew this, so they came after us aggressively. I received calls every few days from top-tier private equity firms like Blackstone and KKR offering positions that promised the potential to make $250,000 for the first year on the job. One of these places was supposed to be the next stop on my path, providing the over-the-top earnings that I had dreamed of as a kid. For my coworkers who weren't interested in those jobs, slots at Harvard's and Stanford's prestigious business school programs awaited.

But I didn't even consider applying to any of those places. I loved what I was doing with PoP and wanted to give it a little more time to see its full potential through. I decided I would stay at Bain through August to complete the third and final year of the associate consultant program, then work full-time for one year on PoP, then determine what would come next.

As right as it seemed to return to my job, an amazing but time-consuming opportunity for PoP had just cropped up. Chase launched its first Community Giving program, which offered donations of up to $1 million to nonprofits that received the most votes through a social media campaign. Social giving was being democratized for the first time, and it couldn't have come at a more opportune moment.

I was not on Twitter, but the Chase Community Giving program gave us the impetus to sign up. A team of ten volunteers took rotations throughout the day to post on PoP's account, interacting directly with every supporter we could find. We had friends change their profile pictures to a graphic we created saying "I voted for PoP" with the URL to the voting page. They created massive Facebook event pages that invited tens of thousands of people to vote on our behalf. After two weeks of campaigning, we made it into the final round.

To prepare, I built a Bain-style Excel model to determine the likely front-runners. It would normally have taken me a day or two to fill in all the data fields (e.g., website rating, Facebook Cause members, Twitter followers), but I enlisted assistance. I put up a Facebook status saying, *Who can spare a few hours to do some virtual volunteer research for PoP?* Within minutes, I had twenty volunteers from California to Cambodia that I could assign five organizations each. Two hours later, I aggregated their collective research and the model was complete. We had crowdsourced our first research project.

The results showed that we'd most likely be able to finish in the top twenty. If we placed first, then we would win $1 million. Second through sixth meant $100,000. All I could think about was funding the third school, and then our fourth, and then our fifth. *Five schools,* I started to think, *that would be crazy.*

As I had expected when I left on my externship, there were no active cases leading into the holidays, so I was tasked with client-development research. When they finally staffed me on a bigger case, I was assigned to work remotely for a manager who was living in Boston. They asked me to complete a detailed analysis of a $3 billion potential client and produce the forty-slide "redbook" that would be used to brief the three senior partners who would be pitching the company.

That same week, the final round of the Chase Community Giving campaign launched. When I started pulling together the deck for the Bain pitch, I felt like pulling out my hair. I emailed my manager to tell her I was too sick to work, but that wasn't why I barely returned her emails for the next ten days. My priorities were elsewhere.

PoP was up against huge organizations with long histories and enormous mailing lists, but Brad worked with me to create a microsite that highlighted and offered prizes to the supporters who referred the most votes. We activated an army of advocates who relentlessly recruited their friends. We hit the number two spot on the opening day of the final round. By tapping into several major blog networks and social media influencers, we stayed in that position for the next three days of the competition.

But in the latter half of the week, bigger organizations grabbed a foothold and pulled ahead. Although we eventually dropped out of the running for the $1 million, we ended up with thirty thousand votes—enough people to fill Madison Square Garden nearly two times. We finished in eleventh place, putting the Pencils of Promise name on the map and winning $25,000—enough to build an entire school.

Our next party filled our coffers even further. Several hundred people showed up for our second annual masquerade event, guaranteeing we would close out the year with enough funds for at least three new schools. We committed to breaking ground on these new schools in Laos, which we aimed to complete by April. We had seen the power of small donations in effect, but for the first time we tasted the tremendous impact of a large donation. Of course it was secured through many small acts—in this case thirty thousand people clicking a button—and it wouldn't have been fitting any other way. Meanwhile, I still had eight long months left at my job. An eternity.

When I was on the road in the RV, Hope Taitz, a mother of three who was extremely active in philanthropy, discovered our organization. She had cofounded an impactful education nonprofit twenty years earlier and was interested in our work. We met for sushi on a chilly January afternoon, and I told her of my conundrum. While PoP was growing beyond my expectations, my work at Bain was suffering immensely and was holding me back from what I wanted to do. For the first time I shared something I hadn't told anyone: "I might want to leave Bain early."

I decided that if we could confidently raise $100,000 that year, I would leave to pursue PoP.

"Hope, I've never asked anybody for anything like this before, but I am asking you for something big," I said. "Can you help raise fifty thousand dollars this year?"

She didn't pause. "I think I can be helpful, but I'm interested in things that are far more important than just raising funds. I'd want to help you build a world-class organization."

I'd found the right partner. She not only offered to help open doors, but she offered to coach me along the way. I saw the opportunity to learn from someone who could mentor me through the next several years while focusing on the best interests of the organization as well.

With Hope on the team, I had confidence that I might be able to pull this off. She was the first person with business legitimacy who was ready to invest time and money into our burgeoning organization. I walked straight back into the Bain office from our lunch and asked an HR manager if we could speak confidentially.

"What would I be giving up if I left Bain now?" I asked. "What are the numbers?"

"Between your salary and bonuses, it would be somewhere around . . ."

When I heard the number, my mouth dropped. *Shit, that's a lot of money*, I thought. *But six months of my life is a lot of time.*

If I waited that long, I wasn't sure what would happen, but I knew that if I left Bain early and fully dedicated myself to PoP, I would be forced to make it succeed. Reid Hoffman, the founder of LinkedIn, has said that an entrepreneur is someone who will "jump off a cliff and assemble an airplane on the way down." I wasn't ready to jump yet, but it was time to start looking for airplane parts.

I began by looking for office space. A friend of mine worked at the commercial real estate firm Cushman & Wakefield and told me about a potential space I might be able to get on the cheap. Norman Belmonte ran a women's-garment business, but his office needs had recently shrunk.

"Norman wants to rent out his space," my friend Ethan told me. "Go talk to him."

We didn't have a website or an annual report, but we did have a "media kit" displaying Nick's recent photos that students from the top design course at Pratt Institute's School of Art & Design had created under Brad's oversight. The pages shared our story and mission, and they looked gorgeous too.

During my lunch break I met Norman at his office on Thirty-second Street and Madison Avenue. As soon as I walked in, he turned away from his AOL account to ask me a direct question: "So what business is it that you want to rent a room from me for?" I had started to refine my pitch during the hundreds of coffee chats over the past year, but this one had to hit home.

Many presentations follow a traditional hero's journey, with the presenter portraying himself or herself as the hero to win over the audience. But the best presentations—the ones that inspire action—are those where the same journey is portrayed, except the audience is the focus. It's not about the presenter; it's about the chance that the audience has to become the hero by completing a well-defined task.

When these presentations are given one-on-one, it's impor-tant to first understand what the other person cares about most. I began by asking what he was passionate about. His words revealed the joy he gained from being a grandfather, and when I looked around the room, I realized we were surrounded by photos of his family. In response, I started explaining my relationship with Ma and how the first school was built to honor her. Then, I showed Norman our beautiful printed media kit, explaining each page with a story detailing the backgrounds of the kids pictured. Finally, I talked about the heavy decision I was facing—whether to leave Bain—and how transformational it would be if PoP could secure a great office space at a low rent. The stage was set for a hero, and Norman could easily step in to fill that role.

"Well, I can't charge you what I wanted to charge you any-more," he said. "I'm the chairman here, so let me talk to my nephew who runs the day-to-day business and get back to you. But I want to help."

By the time I got back to the office, I found an alarming email waiting in my inbox. It was from Dave, the new staffing manager at Bain. *Adam, we need to speak. Please come into my office.*

What he said was not that surprising: "We get that you are passionate about Pencils of Promise, but you need to be a responsible employee. You haven't been working very hard. I hear you called in sick for almost two weeks?"

"I was sick."

"C'mon, not for two weeks." He could see right through me.

"Okay, but I haven't been put on a real case. If you just gave me a consistent client to work on, I don't think this would be an issue."

"Great, I have a case assignment for you. A large university is restructuring its budget and you'll lead the analysis. You'll have to be in upstate New York four days a week for the next four months."

I didn't see that coming. "What if I don't take it?"

"Then you don't stay at Bain."

"Can I think about it?"

"It starts Monday, let me know tomorrow."

"Can I have the weekend?" I was headed to San Francisco with Matt, my childhood friend who had seen me through so much over the years, and with whom I'd not so long ago traveled in Guatemala. He would be the perfect person to help talk me through such a big decision.

"Yes."

James De La Vega is a famed street artist in New York City, known for the chalk drawings, murals, and message-based graffiti that he leaves across the East Village. Some of his works have been auctioned at Christie's, and some get washed away by the morning rain. As I walked home to my new apartment on Tenth Street that evening, wrestling with the decision Dave had asked me to make, I found a large cardboard box left as garbage next to my front steps. De La Vega must also have walked by this box moments before I arrived, because it was now freshly painted in his trademark bold, black letters with three of his most well-known words: *Become Your Dream.*

In certain situations you ask to see a sign to guide you in the right direction. Sometimes these calls to a higher power are answered, and sometimes we are left to seek counsel from within. But if you look for them, the signs will usually present themselves to those with open eyes. This was one of those moments when the sign could not have been clearer. My answer was literally written by my front steps. As the snow began to fall later that night, I rushed outside to cut the words out of the box, vowing that one day when we opened a PoP office, I would hang this sign for others to use as guidance as well. But I still had no idea where that office would be.

As I headed to the airport the next day, I received an email from Norman: *Call me right away.*

After making it through security, I called him from the gate. "I wanted to make sure I spoke to you before you headed out for the weekend," he said. "I spoke to my nephew. We're going to give you a free office space on our floor starting in May or June. You just let me know when you want to start."

That was the final sign I needed. I got on the flight knowing that my mind was made up—I would leave Bain the next week to pursue PoP full-time.

The following week I drafted the scariest email of my life. It began, *To my Bain family, it's been real. It's been great. It's been really great.*

I knew that the moment I sent it out, the four-paragraph email would be delivered to more than four hundred employees across the system—the entire NYC office, international partners, managers, mentors, and friends. I would be notifying them that I was leaving the company, and there would be no turning back.

Nearly everyone I knew, including my own parents, thought I was an idiot to do this. We didn't have a single full-time employee or major institutional donor. Every part of my rational brain told me to stay and finish out my time. It was safe, it was lucrative, and it was easy. But I couldn't ignore the voice somewhere deep inside that knew what I needed to do. In some ways it felt like a choice, and in other ways it felt as if I was simply following the path I was meant to take. The signs were clear. I took a deep breath, packed up my desk, and pressed send.

※

CREATE SEPARATION
TO BUILD CONNECTION

Norman's office space would not be ready for a few months, so until the summer arrived, I lived and worked in my 350-square-foot East Village apartment. When people asked, "My office or yours?" I always responded with "Let's go for a quick bite instead." I'd then suggest a café within three blocks of my apartment so I could pop out and then return to my workstation, also known as my couch. Sometimes you have to fake it until you make it, and this was definitely one of those times.

After removing my TV and other distractions, I nailed a huge whiteboard to the wall to map out any ideas that came to mind. I was as single as it gets, but it felt like I was in a relationship with Pencils of Promise. From the moment I woke up until my head hit the pillow at night, 99 percent of my time and mental energy was spent on the organization. Failure was not an option, so I made sure I was always connected via my phone or computer, in case that next big email was about to come through.

Not long into my new round-the-clock work regimen, a compelling opportunity came up. On an international flight, I sat next to some of the founders of Summit Series, a company that hosted exclusive retreats for young entrepreneurs, artists, and activists. They focused on business practices, tech innovation, and networking. The idea was to mash up the greatest group of multidiscipline world changers—entrepreneurs, scientists, venture capitalists, entertainers, and media people—and see what good they can do.

Throughout the flight, I talked with Josh and Jeff from the Summit founding team. By the time we arrived, Jeff told me confidently, "We are going to change your life." They invited me to attend their next major event in Washington, DC, which came with the hefty price tag of $3,600.

We definitely couldn't afford that, but when I looked at the website, I saw that the list of speakers and attendees was incredibly impressive. Not only were luminaries such as former president Bill Clinton and Ted Turner speaking, but many of the nonprofit founders I admired most would be there as well. We needed to add some firepower to our board of directors, and this event would be attended by hundreds of the types of people I was looking for. "I'll come if you can give me a significant nonprofit discount and introduce me to three people who will join my board," I said.

"Done," Josh replied. "Also, flights are cheap."

"Don't worry. I'll be taking the bus," I said. No way would I spend the extra money on a plane ticket. I didn't even take money out of PoP to get myself health insurance—something that would later prove to be disastrous.

*   *   *

I knew that we didn't have the money to pay a second employee, but I also knew that without a team the organization couldn't scale. My plan wasn't perfect, but I started to recruit a small army of high school and college volunteer interns to work on PoP all summer for free. With the economy in such bad shape, I figured I could even find someone between jobs who might volunteer as a full-time intern manager as well. After posting these positions on several message boards, I started to get a few decent résumés.

One applicant in particular really stood out, Jocelyn Kmet, a former recruiter at McKinsey & Company, who began her letter, "Dear Hiring Manager." As I sat alone in my apartment reading that header, I couldn't help but laugh. If only she knew how small our organization really was.

Although I had to fly to Laos the next day for the opening of three new schools, I decided to meet with her at my corner Starbucks a few hours before heading to the airport. Spunky, stylish, and smart, she was clearly qualified for the job. She had personality and passion, but I left believing that I should wait to interview a few more candidates before pulling the trigger. I thanked her for her time, then rushed off to the airport.

When I arrived in Luang Prabang, I was welcomed at Rattana Guesthouse with big hugs from Leslie and Lanoy. After catching up briefly, I headed to Joma to check emails. The cashier rang up the freshly squeezed orange juice that I ordered, and when I asked for the Wi-Fi password, she handed me a thin, one-inch-wide piece of paper. It looked like the scrolls used inside fortune cookies, and when I read the password printed on the back, I could barely believe what I saw.

The password was *jocelyn9*.

The signs couldn't have been any clearer. I decided to follow the fates, and the first email I wrote was to Jocelyn offering her the job. She accepted right away and started recruiting the team that would become our first intern class.

When I returned stateside, I met with Jocelyn to outline a work plan and then headed down to Washington, DC, to attend my first Summit Series event. A collection of 750 of the nation's leading young entrepreneurs had come together to connect and trade ideas. I recognized many names and companies on the attendee list, but had never before met a single person there.

I was committed to making the most of every second, so I signed up for both of the optional "speed networking" sessions offered as part of the preconference programming. I was used to having hour-long coffee chats where I told my story in twenty minutes, but suddenly I was forced to explain PoP in less than sixty seconds. In those two sessions I met the founders of eighty emerging startups who were just as eager to get their name out there, including the entrepreneurs behind Airbnb, a company now worth billions. All of these founders demonstrated one thing in particular: they could tell their story fast.

Later that night I went to a party where I met Jason Russell, Laren Poole, and Bobby Bailey, the three cofounders of Invisible Children, an organization I revered. They had won the $1 million grand prize in the Chase Community Giving Contest. When I introduced myself to Laren at the bar, he pulled in Jason right away, shouting, "This is the guy from Pencils of Promise. When you were in second place, right away we were so scared, everyone in our organization was asking, 'Who the hell are these guys!'" PoP had never paid a dollar to advertise itself, but its social media presence was clearly paying off. I couldn't believe three guys I admired from afar actually knew who I was.

Leaders from every red-hot start-up were in attendance, and whether people were onstage or in the audience, they clearly all shared the same general path. Most had been told no, but they refused to give up. They were confident and unflappable, but they weren't afraid to ask for help. And they had all failed at times. But they learned more from their mistakes than their successes.

Those I met defined themselves by what was on their mind, not on their business card. And although I felt like the new kid on the block, I was glad to be around people with so much accumulated experience and wisdom to share.

Ironically, the one person I didn't have much time to connect with was my assigned roommate, Adam Witty, who founded and ran a publishing company in South Carolina. We barely crossed paths until the final morning as we were both packing to go. When he asked me what I did, I hit him with my newly refined sixty-second pitch.

"That's really great," he replied. "Our company's five-year anniversary is coming up in a few months. How about we ask all of our authors to donate to Pencils of Promise and build a new school together? I'll put you in touch with Brooke from my team now; we'll make this happen."

Through this one quick conversation, I had locked in my first full-school commitment. Over the next several months and years, members of the Summit community would fund many, many more schools. Some of them used their companies to build a school, a few wrote checks from their personal accounts, and others simply put me on an email with someone they knew was interested in our work. And through that community, I met three people who would ultimately join our board of directors.

As I rode the bus back to my cramped East Village apartment, I thought about how important it was for me to occasionally and deliberately separate from my normal routine. The meaningful connections I'd had over the previous few days didn't happen when I was staring at my computer, banging out emails, but when I focused on being present with the people right in front of me. I began to think, *How many times have I missed an incredible connection that could have been made because I had my face in my phone instead of paying attention to those around me?*

I also thought back to my college basketball days, and remembered that muscles are not strengthened as you are lifting weights. In fact, lifting heavy weights actually creates small tears that slightly damage your muscles. But through the act of recovery, your body repairs these small tears in ways that help your muscles grow in size and strength. In other words, the recovery period is just as essential as the working period if you want to be a peak performer.

This realization led me to institute a personal policy of going off email from Friday night until Sunday morning. I would use my weekends to rest, rejuvenate, and reconnect with those I cherished most. For one day a week, it's important to allow yourself to be a human being, rather than a human doing.

Little did I know that three weeks later, my new policy would be tested by a man in Fort Lauderdale who could potentially provide the biggest donation in the history of Pencils of Promise.

And he wanted to talk through the weekend.

NEVER TAKE NO FROM
SOMEONE WHO CAN'T SAY YES

To grow and scale we needed to craft a unique digital presence, but we still didn't have a website. For over a year we had a placeholder that read, *Website coming soon.*

We simply didn't have the resources to invest in a website. It would have taken a significant amount of time and money to do it right, and I decided to wait until we could afford it. Your website is your storefront, your billboard, and your calling card. It's the focal part of any modern business, and I was determined to create one that stood out.

One of the biggest challenges of the nonprofit space is the false perception that "overhead," or anything other than your core programs, consists of inefficient, careless spending. But investment in your infrastructure is essential for growth. A strong website should be the flagship asset of a good organization, especially one like ours that works in remote parts of the world. Still, donors want to see a high ratio of spending on programs to overhead (traditionally 80 percent is considered very good), so I had to anxiously wait for a miracle before I could justify spending real money on a website.

Brad was still working at BBH but was functioning as our de facto chief branding officer. He reached out to our mutual friend Alex. We used to play basketball together growing up, and now he worked at AgencyNet, one of the top digital agencies in the country. Considering they built Bacardi's site and the Clinton Foundation's, it seemed like a joke that they would even talk to us. We'd never be able to pay for the services. But maybe Alex could provide some advice or volunteer some time to recruit and quarterback a team of freelancers to build our site. At least that's what I hoped for in my wildest dreams.

After a bit of research, I allocated a budget of $20,000 to build our website. I agonized over spending that amount on anything besides a new school, but this was an investment in our future and one that could pay off exponentially. Unfortunately, Brad told me the minimum for a good site would be $100,000.

Alex and I arranged a lunch to catch up, during which I gave him the refined pitch on what PoP was doing. In the past year we had worked with local partners to break ground on five schools in Laos and two in Nicaragua. We aimed to break ground on ten more while building a movement of over one hundred thousand supporters before the year ended.

The conversation just flowed and I could tell Alex was interested in what we were doing. By the end of the hour he said, "I'm in. I'd be more than happy to help. If you have twenty thousand dollars to spend, it'll be tight, but maybe I can get some guys to work pro bono and others to commit at reduced fees."

I was ecstatic. As we walked to the door, he mentioned one other idea that came to mind. "Our CEO is a really philanthropic guy. I think you'd get along well. There's even a chance we could take this project on at the agency level, but let me talk to Rich. He's based in Fort Lauderdale but comes to New York City often, so maybe I can get you a meeting. In any case, count me in."

That was promising news, but we wanted the website up and running by summer. It was already April.

I let two weeks go by and emailed Alex: *Any word from Rich?*
Still working on it, he replied.

Several more weeks went by. Jocelyn and I moved into our one-room space in Norman's office, but I still hadn't heard back from Alex about getting a meeting with Rich. Worse, we hadn't made any progress on our freelancer search because we were holding out for the small chance that AgencyNet would take us on.

I knew that although his intentions were good, Alex didn't have the authority to mobilize AgencyNet on our behalf. You'll often hear people say, "I'm sorry, I wish I could." That's code for "I don't have the authority to give you the answer you want." Never take no from someone who can't say yes. Rich was the only person who could give me the answer I was looking for, so I had to do whatever it took to meet with him in person or catch him on the phone.

After twenty-two emails with Alex to set up an in-person meeting with Rich on a Tuesday afternoon, Rich had to cancel and return early to Fort Lauderdale. Drastic measures were in order. Sometimes you have to show someone that you're willing to run through a wall before they'll open the front door.

I emailed Alex to tell him that if Rich was anywhere close to a major airport in the next two weeks, I would fly there to meet him. I figured a flight would cost $300—a big expense in my mind—but I knew the website was the most important thing to PoP's growth going forward.

Less than two hours later Alex wrote back, *Rich will be calling you at 4:30 p.m. today.*

At 4:00 p.m. I got a text: *This is Rich from AgencyNet. Can we speak at 5?*

Sure, I replied. I was not accustomed to talking to CEOs, let alone texting with them. But I realized his approach was genius— if it didn't go well, I still didn't have his email address so I would never contact him again.

Just before 5:00 p.m. I walked into a spare room in Norman's office and brought a three-foot-tall photo of Nuth that we had printed on poster board for our events. It showed the world's most adorable child sitting barefoot on the steps of the Pha Theung school, tilting her head to the side and looking straight into the camera lens. She seemed to be looking out from the photo, asking playfully, *Whaddya got?* Before I called Rich, I put the photo on the chair across from me in the empty, dimly lit conference room. I would look at Nuth while I was talking. She would help me stay focused on what mattered most.

He picked up on the first ring. "Hey, Adam, it sounds like you are doing pretty cool stuff." Rich sounded much less formal and much more authentic than I anticipated.

I spent the next forty minutes walking Rich through what we did. Instead of asking the usual questions about the logistics of each school, such as "How do you find the teachers?" (the education ministry provides them and we help train them), he asked probing, insightful questions about organizational health: "What's your biggest fear?" "What's your board makeup?" "What are your biggest challenges to growth?"

Rich seemed genuinely interested in what we were doing, and he seemed cool as hell. We were getting along great. But I knew he'd already given me a lot of time, and I had to get to the point.

"Rich, part of the reason why I wanted to talk to you is that we need to build a website. I wanted to know if maybe you guys would be able to build it"—I could hear myself nervously stumbling over my own words—"at a reduced rate of twenty thousand dollars?" *I can't believe I just asked that*, I thought. This was my first outright big ask on behalf of Pencils of Promise. My heart was beating out of my chest.

"Well, Adam, to tell you the truth, I am not involved in the production side, so I'll have to talk to the VP of production." *Damn.* "But I'm already thinking bigger. Give me a few days. Maybe we can chat on Monday."

What was he thinking? He texted me his email address, and I followed up with a thank-you note the following night, which was a Thursday. He responded Friday afternoon: *Loved our convo. You around this weekend for a chat?*

Yup, I'm around all weekend. Just let me know what works best for you, I wrote back right away. But as the hours crept toward Friday night, I had to decide whether I would check my email for his response throughout the weekend and break my new policy or keep the policy in place. Should I make an exception? Or stick to what I'd determined? Would he think I was rude if I ignored his email, or would he consider me lazy if I told him about my recent decision to go off email once a week? I decided to preempt the conflict and lay out the honest truth. I called him just before sundown Friday night:

"I just want to be open with you. I recently put a practice into place where I go off email from sundown Friday to Sunday morning, to make sure I stop working and spend quality time with my loved ones. I also find it makes me more energized for the next week ahead if I'm not on email over the weekend, and it helps to avoid burnout."

I held my breath. Would he think I was a slacker who didn't work hard? So many people wear their 24-7 work hours like a badge of honor.

"Adam, I respect that. If I could do that, I would do it too. I'm glad you told me. Let's chat next week."

Sure enough, Rich texted me Monday at 9:30 a.m.: *Can we chat? I'll give you a call in 15 minutes.*

I put my earbuds in and paced back and forth throughout the apartment. Finally, the phone rang.

"Listen, I thought a lot about this over the weekend and I also spoke to my VP of production. There are three things I'd like to offer you. First, we are not going to do your website for twenty thousand dollars." My heart sank. "Instead I've already approved one hundred and fifty thousand dollars in pro bono resources for us to build you a top-notch website free of charge."

I couldn't believe it. My frantic pacing turned into psychotic sprinting and fist pumping in my tiny apartment.

"Second, I'd like to join your board of directors, if you'll have me. And third, one of my friends, Jay, is the president of another leading digital agency and is looking for something to help him find more meaning in his life. Will you speak to him? He might want to join your board too." While Rich spoke, I was still running the length of my apartment silently screaming, *Yessssssss!* over and over.

I composed myself before responding, mainly because I was completely out of breath. The board was still informal, just me and five of my friends in their midtwenties who had helped start and build PoP: Mimi, Brad, Mike, Libbie, and Jen. I was hoping to bring on Hope and a director at Bain, Karen Harris, who had read my farewell email and reached out about getting more involved. I imagine most people would jump at the chance to have Rich and his friend on our board as well, but I couldn't just say yes without consulting the team.

"First off I can't thank you enough for all three of your offers. There are six of us on the current board, and I would need to talk with the others before I could make any commitments. But I'm definitely very interested in you joining. In terms of the website, though, count us one hundred percent in."

"I'm glad you take the others on your board into account. I'll be in New York next week. Let's go out to dinner so we can meet in person."

"Absolutely, I'd love that."

As soon as we hung up, I called Brad and then Alex to tell them the great news. We had started in hopes of getting a group of free-lancers to build our site for $20,000 and now had one of the top digital agencies in the country putting its full weight behind us at no cost. The feeling of elation was extraordinary.

The next week, Rich and I grabbed dinner together, and Alex joined us for a celebratory drink. It was too early to know then, but Rich would not only build our website and join our board of directors, he would guide me in the months ahead through one of the biggest decisions of my life.

STAY GUIDED BY YOUR VALUES, NOT YOUR NECESSITIES

John Nolan, a friend of my father's who had known me since I was a child, was one of the wealthiest people I had ever met. After launching a successful Wall Street brokerage house in the 1980s, he moved to Greenwich to start a series of investment funds. We'd always hit it off, and when I was nineteen, I spent the summer working for him as he launched a fund of funds. "You'll go on and do big things," he'd said.

A few months after I left Bain and was working on PoP full-time, John called me out of the blue. "I have an idea for a business. I want to meet with you."

This was a curveball, and an intriguing one, but I was set on what I was doing. "Thanks for thinking of me, but I'm working on the nonprofit I started."

"Just come out and meet with me," boomed John in his husky voice.

I always liked and respected John as a person, and as a successful financier and businessman. So I took the train out to Greenwich. When I remarked to the receptionist how nice the office looked, she told me to tell John. He owned the entire building. As soon as I sat down with him, he asked me an unexpected question. "What do you know about the e-commerce auction business?"

"Nothing."

He tossed a thick, printed presentation across the mahogany desk to me. "You need to learn it fast," he responded emphatically.

I skimmed through the pages. Websites were auctioning off items, usually coveted electronics like iPads, flat-screen TVs, and cameras. Customers actively bid online at below-market prices, but through clever auction and pricing mechanisms, companies could find ways to make huge profits while selling goods at a huge discount. Dozens of companies were rapidly entering this new space, each pursuing a uniquely competitive path.

"Adam, I don't know about technology or modern branding, but I know this seems like a great business with an incredible financial model. These companies are practically printing money! I'm going to start one of these companies, but I need someone young and ambitious who understands the Web to build it. You'll be the cofounder and CEO."

"I'm working on Pencils of Promise right now."

"Do it on the side. I run my kids' baseball program on the side. I'm fine if you work on your charity after hours, but you need to work full-time out of my office here in Greenwich."

"Even if I did take this on, it would require a reverse commute from the city."

"I'll have a black town car take you to and from your apartment every day. You'll have a six-figure salary and you'll get equity. Of course you'll have full health insurance too."

It was all incredibly attractive.

"Put together a budget for the capital you'd need to launch the company. Staff, travel, expense account, whatever you need. I'll personally arrange financing for the whole thing," John continued.

"What range are you thinking to start?"

"Make it around a million dollars," he replied without hesitation. "Plus, I'll give you the entire floor upstairs."

I thought of my Pencils of Promise team made up entirely of volunteer interns at our tiny one-room space in Norman's office sitting around a used IKEA table. John was describing a very different operation.

"Let me have a few days to think this all over. But there's one more thing: I only want to work on businesses that create social good."

"No problem, as long as it makes a lot of money. And you've got to remove all those damn strings from your wrists."

In Laos, special occasions are celebrated through a beautiful tradition called a *baci* (pronounced *ba-see*) ceremony. Laotians believe that thirty-two spirit guardians watch over and protect each person. Occasionally these spirits wander away from us, leaving us vulnerable and imbalanced, so in times of significance and celebration Laotians tie white thread around each other's wrists to bind the protective spirits to each other and to bring peace, harmony, and good fortune. Baci ceremonies celebrate weddings and births, and, as we found out, school openings.

By the time we finished the fourth and fifth school openings in the villages of Pak Pa and Xienglohm, my wrists were covered in white cotton string. I looked like a boxer training for a fight. It's customary to let the threads fall off on their own. They can be untied, but are not supposed to be cut off.

John was referring to the strings that had been tied on my

wrists at the opening of a new school in the village of Bo He, one of the poorest in Luang Prabang Province. During the ceremony I sat on the floor between Leslie and Lanoy, and afterward we rode along a dirt road to return to the city of Luang Prabang. I drove my motorbike as I had hundreds of times before, cruising along the dusty gravel, but driving much faster than I should have been. As the dirt road ended and I neared the turnoff for the highway, I suddenly saw a local girl on a motorbike coming right toward me. I swerved to avoid a major collision, and my bike slid out from underneath me, sending me flying headfirst over the handlebars.

Big potholes dominated the connecting road, and I landed in one, crushing my left shoulder and gashing open my hand. Lanoy rushed to help me, but the damage was already done. My shoulder had been torn from the socket. By the time I returned stateside the following week, my shoulder was in excruciating pain, loudly cracking and popping with every minor movement. I needed surgery as soon as possible.

But I had opted out of health insurance when my coverage ended through Bain. I hadn't wanted to drain PoP's resources unless medical attention was imminently necessary, and now I was stuck because no individual-insurance provider would take me because of my preexisting shoulder injury. Suddenly, John's offer gave me a way out by joining his company's group plan.

I started to spend my mornings and evenings exploring his idea. I began by creating a model that donated money to a cause through every item sold. The company would be able to give back, and every person who bid could contribute to charity too.

Meanwhile, I continued going to the PoP office, working with Jocelyn and the interns. We were planning weekly fundraisers while creating a curriculum of sanitation, health, and nutrition lessons for the children attending our schools. In the shadows, I began to build out John's idea on the side. I created a logo and started working with Israeli contractors to design the site. John was courting me hard and trying to make it official. "Do whatever the hell you want with PoP in your spare time," he said, "but our company should be your focus."

John had thrown a potentially lucrative opportunity in my lap. We both believed it would be a cash cow. If the company took off, I could potentially make millions in months off the equity alone. And philanthropy, something I cared deeply about, was built into the business. But the motivation would undeniably be the dollars, not the social impact.

Meanwhile, everything at PoP was finally taking off: I had an office, a staff, and a website on the way. How could I build two companies simultaneously? I knew that I needed to pick one and go all in.

I was tormented by the weight of this decision. Every day I went back and forth on which to choose. When I told my parents that I thought I would work on PoP instead of joining forces with John, my dad shouted, "What's wrong with you!" They weren't alone in their thinking. Every single person that I sought counsel from told me I should join John. I ultimately decided that his offer was too good to turn down and told him that I'd come out to Greenwich in a few days to sign the paperwork.

But I never made peace with it. I had spent the past week collaborating with Rich on the website, and one night, over dinner, I told him about John's offer and asked for his thoughts on whether I could build PoP and another company simultaneously.

"I only have one question for you," he began. "Can you be in love with two girls at the same time?"

"What do you mean?"

"There are people who can be completely in love with two different women at the same time; there are others who say they can only love one. Which are you?"

"Well, I know myself pretty well, and I can only be in love with one person at a time."

"That's your answer. Pick the one you truly love."

I knew in that moment exactly which one I had to pick. We had only recently met, but I was so grateful to have found someone who could help me wade through the contradicting voices in my head.

I didn't sleep at all the night before I went to sign my operating agreement with John. The paperwork would make me CEO and grant me a salary, equity, and benefits. Between the money and the health insurance, I could cover all of my immediate needs.

But I'd have to change everything I stood for. You never realize how much you value something until you are faced with the prospect of losing it. And you never know your selling price until someone makes you a hard offer. I stayed up through sunrise, furiously scribbling in my journal, sealing my decision in ink on the final pages.

I took the train out to Greenwich and told John that I couldn't accept the job. I was going to stick with PoP. I knew if I wanted any success, I had to devote myself to it fully. When you're part of something special, you have to cherish it and defend it against many outside distractions and temptations. But nothing is more potent or deceptive than the competing interests of another great opportunity. In those moments when priorities clash, always stay guided by your values, not your perceived necessities. Necessities exist in a state of mind that will not last, whereas values are transcendent and enduring. I understood that I might fail, but I wouldn't let it happen because I changed my compass along the way.

YOU CANNOT
FAKE AUTHENTICITY

For nearly eighteen months PoP had been run exclusively by volunteers. I'd had so much fun collaborating with my friends on something meaningful, but the organization was rapidly attracting new donors, and we needed to transition from a leadership team of people working with us on the side to those working fulltime at the organization. The growth of early-stage companies is highly dependent on how much time you can spend on the entity, and with more funds coming in we had the opportunity to evolve from an army of volunteers and evangelists into a legitimate team of experts and ninjas.

But where could I find these people? I considered posting on job boards for certain positions, including someone to manage our financials and another person to lead the staff day to day while I was traveling and building relationships. But I was too impatient to sit around and hope for the right résumé to show up, so I decided to be proactive rather than reactive. I began aggressively recruiting key individuals for a small team. The two things I cared most about were passion and talent. Everything else could be taught or learned.

I began my recruiting mission by looking to my circle of friends. I knew that every person on my Semester at Sea ship had backpacked through areas of profound poverty, often spending days in rural villages and gaining deep appreciation for and insights into the developing world. Many had forged academic and career paths focused on addressing social issues. My friend Jill had worked with multiple global NGOs and was finishing a double master's degree on nonprofit management and human rights. She agreed to become the point person to liaise with our in-country staff. My friend Hoolie was finishing four years as a management consultant at Deloitte and was planning to extern at the Clinton Global Initiative for the summer before heading to Dartmouth for his MBA. I persuaded him to extern at PoP instead, and after a month in Laos where he helped Leslie and Lanoy build the first completely independent school (hiring our own architects, builders, and staff), I offered him the job as our chief operating officer.

"Come on, you'll never get another opportunity like this in your life," I urged him, trying to appeal to his inner entrepreneur. "You'll build an organization from the ground up, lead all staff, and educate thousands in the process."

"You know how badly I want this," he replied. "My fiancée will kill me if I defer business school any longer, but I've secretly been interviewing for doorman positions so I can do this while working nights to supplement my income."

I was amazed. This guy worked for one of the most prestigious consulting firms in the world and was accepted into Dartmouth's

MBA program, but he was looking for doorman jobs so he could work at PoP. I never doubted his talent, but now his passion blew me away too.

"I'll tell you what," he continued. "I'll take the job, but only if you promise that you won't try to persuade me to stay any longer than one year, because you know I will."

"Deal." I extended my hand to shake on it. I had a COO—and one that I believed in just as much as he believed in me.

I desperately wanted to bring on someone from the Bain network to instill a focus on results across the organization, so when I received an email from Emily Gore, who was widely regarded as one of the superstars in the class below me, I met with her right away. She was looking for an externship that gave her international experience. I made her an offer on the spot and she agreed to join for six months, creating robust monitoring and evaluation programs (referred to as M&E in nonprofit lingo) around our work in Laos.

Our international operations there were growing rapidly under Leslie's guidance, but we were having trouble expanding in Nicaragua. Due to bad roads and low population density, we were spending far more per build while reaching fewer students than expected. We were committed to supporting the schools we built in Nicaragua for the long term, but I urged the team to consider expansion to the Lake Atitlán region in Guatemala, an area that I knew well from my days with Joel Puac. The need there was tremendous. If we were to grow rapidly in the region, though, we would need someone with experience to guide our work there. Once again, rather than looking for a random leader, I turned to someone I knew and trusted.

My childhood friend Noah had, since graduating from

college, worked in Ethiopia, Sudan, and Bolivia for a large NGO. When I reached out, he was living in Bolivia while advising on a multimillion-dollar national health-care project. He explained to me how restricted he felt by rigid, bureaucratic grants that didn't allow him to address the most important issues that those they were trying to support were facing. I saw he had both unique passion and talent for global-development work, and I recruited him hard. At our mutual friend's wedding I slipped him a PoP presentation detailing our programs and told him to interview with Hoolie the following week. Two months later Noah moved to Lake Atitlán to become our Latin American regional director.

As the team started to grow both internationally and at home, our office situation in New York started to present some significant challenges. Norman had offered us one room in the back of his office, which we filled with ten to twenty interns every day, and we had shared access to the showroom to use as a conference room. Since I couldn't conduct major meetings with staff crowded all around, I had to meet with potential donors and heads of companies in the shared showroom space. Since Norman's company sold ladies' apparel, the showroom showcased its line of women's underwear. The walls were completely lined with granny panties. During in-depth conversations with major donors and partners, rather than looking at me, they'd be gawking at the oversize underwear hanging over my shoulder. It was awfully hard to be taken seriously with extra-large pink bloomers all around.

Our panty problem was solved when Mimi left her job in commercial real estate at the end of the summer to join PoP full-time and, as a departing gift, her boss offered us an amazing deal on an eight-hundred-square-foot space in the Lower East Side that contained a large room and an attached conference room separated by a sliding glass door.

This space became our first independent office, and we vowed to uphold a PoP company culture that was true to us. I wrote eight office rules the night before moving in and read them aloud on our first day. Rule #1 set the tone for the type of staff we would recruit: "Hopeless idealism in things that are utterly impossible is required to work here. If you want to be realistic, please work elsewhere. This is a place for dreamers." Rule #3 stated the importance of staying humble and asking for help. Rule #4 was to recognize how your energy affected all others around you, and Rule #7 stressed the importance of bringing family (especially grandparents) to the office so you could share your work with those who got you there.

I wanted to create a dynamic environment in which all could express themselves and make others better. Every person was required to create a quarterly playlist of their favorite songs, which had to be included in their email signature. You can learn far more about a person from the music he or she listens to than you can from the number of followers he or she has on social media. I also insisted that music be played in the office at all times to keep energy high, and that since most of the staff were unpaid, they'd get compensated in meaningful experiences. Through a Lunch and Learn policy, they spent time with accomplished CEOs to hear about their lives and personal paths. They met with every leader I met with. Soon our office bustled with more than twenty committed, passionate interns, part-time and full-time staff members who lived and breathed PoP.

The final play in building the team was to hire someone who could handle all legal and financial matters—something we needed to ensure trust and accountability across our staff, board, and supporters. Brad had reconnected me to Tom Casazzone, whom I only remembered as my brother's best friend in kindergarten. He now had a legal degree along with experience in nonprofit accounting. Tom began handling the organization's finances, and we soon made it official with a real position and salary.

I was no longer on my own. We had people across the globe who could deliver on our new goal to break ground on our fifteenth school by the end of the year. Our entire leadership team was made up of individuals whom I had known not just as colleagues, but also as friends. Creating a company means you're going to go through hell and high water along the way. You need to know the character of the people at your side. Trust is everything.

While I was building PoP, my brother, Scott, had also changed course and was embarking on a new path as well. He had moved to Atlanta to attend Emory University, where he adopted the nickname I had jokingly given him in high school, Scooter, and quickly built up a business as the biggest nightclub promoter in the city. He transitioned from nightlife to the music industry by working for music mogul Jermaine Dupri at So So Def Recordings, then left college and the label to start his own company managing artists he discovered. His first breakout act was Asher Roth with the number one single "I Love College." One day Scott called me to tell me about his newest act: "He's just a kid, he's only thirteen years old. I found him on YouTube, but he's unbelievable. I'll be in New York next week, so I'll bring him by your apartment so you guys can meet."

One week later, a tiny kid with shaggy hair walked into my apartment carrying a guitar that seemed way too big for his body. "Hey, I'm Justin. Can I play you a song?" he asked right away.

"Sure," I said, and over the next twenty minutes he belted out song after song. His voice was absolutely incredible, but his infectious energy won me over even more. You just couldn't help but love this adorable kid. That night when I saw Brad for drinks, I gushed about my brother's new artist.

"He just signed this kid, and he's going to be huge. His name is Justin Bieber."

Because Justin was so young, Scott wasn't just his manager; he also helped raise him. As a result, over the next few years Justin became a part of our extended family. He'd spend days off at my parents' house playing in the pool, practicing dance moves in the mirror, and challenging us to games of one-on-one in the driveway.

I'll never forget the summer afternoon when we were teaching him how to wakeboard, and his first single, "One Time," came on Z100, the largest radio station in the country. It was the first time we had heard it on air, and we all jumped out of our seats, celebrating the moment while Justin sang along at the top of his lungs.

By the time we got back to the house, we had settled down a bit and Justin asked me what I was working on lately. It was the first time we spoke in depth about PoP. Much to my surprise, the mission resonated with him right away.

"This is awesome. I've always wanted to build schools for kids. Scooter, we should do something with Pencils of Promise!" he shouted.

"I think you need to figure out your career first," I said in all seriousness. One song on the radio was great, but he wasn't a global star quite yet. "If you become big, I have no doubt we'll all be able to build many, many schools together."

From the start, Scott stressed the importance of giving back in everything he and Justin did, but Scott purposely didn't pressure Justin to support PoP just because his brother had started the organization. But the organization was focused on empowering young people to realize the changes they could make in the world, and that message was something Justin believed in deeply. He soon became one of the first members of our growing youth movement by helping raise money for the organization and advocating for us on social media. Part of that was due to the closeness of our relationship, but an even bigger part of it was due to the natural alignment of our mission with what he cared about most—helping children.

He was so invested in our work that when the father of one of his fans asked what it would cost for his daughter to meet him before a show, Justin turned to Scott and asked how much it would cost to build a new classroom. Scott replied, "Ten thousand dollars." Justin said, "I'll do it, but only if he donates that money to Pencils of Promise." Later that night, he texted me, *Just built a new classroom for the kids!*

Toward the end of 2010, we planned a family vacation to Africa to meet the families of Sam and Cornelio, our adopted Mozambican brothers. Justin had become a major celebrity by then and was considered one of the biggest pop stars in the world. He wasn't exactly living the life of a normal teenager, so my parents and his mom, Pattie, figured a family vacation without extensive security dictating his every step would be good for him. Scott roomed with his girlfriend, my sister roomed solo, and that left Justin and me as roommates for the two-week trip.

PoP had finally secured the group health insurance coverage needed for me to get shoulder surgery, which I had done as soon as the paperwork allowed, but it left me pretty immobile throughout the trip. Although the pandemonium around Justin wasn't quite as crazy as it was stateside, even in Africa it was still tough for him to walk in the streets without being recognized. Our solution was to spend a lot of time hanging out in the room. We were already close, but with so many hours together we bonded over music, girls, and conversations about how young people like us could help other young people around the world. We also shared plenty of laughs while pranking one another (he'd hack my Twitter account in the morning, and I'd put grapes in his pockets in the afternoon) and trying to avoid the attention drawn by his famous Bieber haircut.

One day in the hotel elevator, two Mozambican women in their midthirties recognized him. They were beside themselves, asking for pictures and autographs.

"You're him!" they exclaimed.

"Who?" he asked calmly.

"You're Justin Bieber!"

"No, I'm not. We just look similar," he insisted, trying to avoid their hysterics.

"Look at your hair. I know that hair. You're you!"

"No! I'm not me!" he exclaimed. Right away, all four of us cracked up, laughing at the blunder. He graciously took a picture with the two women and we headed back to our room. We talked about how excited they were to meet him and started to contemplate how we could use that desire to do some good. A few days later, we got into a serious brainstorming session.

"Let's do something big," Justin said. "Something that'll raise a ton of money and build a bunch of schools."

"How about we create a fundraising contest. Students could compete against each other to see who can raise the most for PoP. Whoever raises the most would get a big grand prize. Maybe you would go visit their school or something?" I asked.

"Nice, let's do that."

"You're sure? You'd have to be willing to fly anywhere in the country to visit the winning school."

"For Pencils of Promise? One hundred percent."

Later that night we recorded a grainy video on my Flip cam. We described a new campaign that we would launch early the next year called Schools4All, which encouraged students to fundraise on behalf of children without access to education, with a chance to win a school visit from Justin. Although the official video we released wouldn't be made until the following April, putting together our first attempt in our room that night was a blast. It didn't feel like some contrived celebrity integration, because it wasn't. The idea came out of a real relationship where both people cared about each other—and the cause.

When we shared the idea the next morning with Scott, he was all for it. "I'm proud of you guys, we can definitely make this happen," he said. You cannot fake authenticity, and since he'd spent his whole life setting the example for both Justin and me to give back to others, on that morning I think he could see his influence taking effect. PoP had its first flagship campaign in the works, we had a trusted team in place, and an inner circle had been established of those who genuinely cared about our work. Now it was finally time for me to let down my guard and start sharing our story with the world.

THERE IS ONLY ONE CHANCE AT A FIRST IMPRESSION

Pencils of Promise was beginning to become known in small circles; we had made a name for ourselves through the Chase Community Giving Contest, had newfound connections at Summit Series, and Justin had begun to amplify our work on Twitter and Facebook. But largely, we stayed out of the traditional press. I knew that the Pencils of Promise story I wanted to tell hadn't yet occurred, so I turned down every interview and media opportunity that came my way.

I cared much more about PoP's long-term success than its early notoriety. Creating something new is easy, creating something that lasts is the challenge. I modeled my approach after the bands I loved most, since many of them had lasted for thirty or forty years. They didn't achieve staying power by splashing their faces across highway billboards as soon as they wrote their first three songs. They first built a loyal base of hard-core fans who felt they "discovered" the band and would ardently share their music with others. Over the years, these bands built up credibility and refined their craft, until they were ready to release a major album. What seemed like an overnight success was actually years in the making.

I'd seen the stories of other NGOs appear in minor and major publications, and while the press helped with visibility, many times it didn't lead to any new funding or support. That's because the single most wasted resource on earth is human intention. How many times have you wanted to do something but not acted right away and forgotten about it later? People probably read those articles and had a strong desire to help in that moment, but the organization didn't have easy and effective mechanisms (website, staff, back-end systems) to convert that intention into action.

I decided early on that we wouldn't share our story through traditional press until we had three pieces in place: (1) what I called a "holy shit" story. You needed to hear about PoP and think, *Holy shit! How have I not heard about this? I need to tell someone else about it now*; (2) a beautiful website with a back-end system to handle inbound inquiries; and (3) the staff and infrastructure to follow up immediately on any interest in our organization.

I waited nearly two years for us to reach a double-digit school count (our "holy shit" story) and get our website, staff, and infrastructure to a place of excellence. By late 2010, we finally had everything in order. AgencyNet delivered a gorgeous website that not only allowed donors to see the exact locations via GPS of schools they funded, but also to take a 360-degree virtual tour inside the classroom using cutting-edge technology. Tom audited our financials and ensured that the most rigorous standards of financial accountability were in effect across all offices. We even added five "adult" board members to guide us through the next period of expected growth. I was finally ready to go outbound with our message.

A reporter had emailed me over the summer to say she wanted to write about Pencils of Promise for the *Huffington Post*. I told her to wait a few months since I still hadn't done a single interview and was waiting for us to break ground on a slew of new schools that fall. But I kept my word that I would go back to her when we were ready. After we did the hour-long interview, she told me that she'd share the piece with her editor and see if they wanted to publish it. Much to my surprise, the article, titled "The New Nonprofit: Pencils of Promise," became the cover story on *HuffPost Impact* over Thanksgiving weekend. The page splashed a huge photo with the catchy teaser "How a Backpacker Built 15 Schools from One Pencil" and was shared nearly twenty-five hundred times, making it the most shared article of its section that month.

This well-timed article put us on the map. The phone started ringing. Emails started coming in. Big brands reached out wanting to work with us. David Yurman's head of global marketing launched a fundraiser in its flagship store and donated products for us to auction off. AOL, *Vogue*, *Variety*, and *People* magazine all reached out to explore ways to partner with us. CBS and ABC started competing to get an exclusive piece on PoP for their evening news programs. The doors to countless major corporate sponsors were now wide open, and I was ready to jump at the opportunity.

Our early beliefs in the value of social media and the rise of cause marketing were finally paying dividends as we began structuring branded partnerships that led to major dollars. Justin's support helped even more, as many of his corporate sponsors donated to PoP because we were his favorite charity (along with the Make-A-Wish Foundation). Justin and Scott even structured the North American leg of the My World Tour to donate $1 per ticket to PoP—creating a new generation of young philanthropists among the fans attending his shows.

In addition to building our relationships with the press and major brands, I also started to focus on speaking at events. The Feast on Good was an invitation-only conference held at the TimesCenter for leading advertising and media execs that focused on driving innovation that makes the world work better. It aimed to bring together what they called "innovators, doers and makers" to dig in and address today's greatest challenges. Brad had been to the event the year before and said it was riveting. "You have to speak there next year," he'd told me.

At the time, that seemed like a pipe dream. We weren't legit enough to speak there—among the likes of established institutions like the *Economist* and Foursquare. But after the *Huffington Post* article, people became aware of us. Brad helped arrange a meeting with Jerri and Michael, the cofounders of the event. "If breakfast goes well, I think they'll ask you to speak," Brad said confidently.

Breakfast at Manhattan's low-key Grey Dog café went great. At the end of almost two hours together, Jerri said, "We are looking for someone young and inspiring as our closing speaker this year. We'd love for you to be it."

"Yeah, for sure." I sounded casual, but I had to restrain myself from getting out of my chair and dancing across the café.

Hours before the speech I was incredibly nervous and consumed with anxiety. I couldn't talk to anyone. I listened to the soothing song "That Western Skyline" by Dawes on repeat on my iPhone and tried to calm myself down. I knew that thousands would be watching on a live stream, including our entire office on the Lower East Side.

The speech was fifteen minutes long, and for the first few I could hear my voice shaking a bit. But when I showed the video of Nuth, Nith, and Tamund, I was reminded of why I was up there and began to speak more confidently. When I finished, many audience members stood up in a standing ovation, and it seemed as though I'd nailed it.

A long line of attendees came up to me to ask questions, swap cards, and share stories. My parents were there, but they patiently waited until I'd addressed everyone else, then finally came up to give me a big hug. For the first time in a while, I felt invincible.

My dad and I embraced, and then he said nonchalantly, "You should look down."

I did and realized my fly was open—it had been open during the entire speech. I couldn't believe it. "Really?"

He nodded and smiled. "Yup."

We both laughed it off, but it was an important reminder to never take oneself too seriously, and to never feel too self-satisfied. The only truth about first impressions is that you only get one. The way people perceive you in those first few moments will set the anchor around which all future interactions are based. Fortunately, few people noticed my blunder, but you can't get those moments back; you can only prepare for making the best possible first impression on those new people you'll meet in the future.

As I left the TimesCenter, I saw several of our staff members who were at the conference mingling with other attendees. Because the staff were wearing PoP T-shirts, people were seeking them out to see how they could get further involved. I couldn't help but smile when I overheard the staff confidently tell others to visit our website, where they could gather all the information they needed to educate a child or fund a school.

Most people rush to get their story out, but by waiting until our "holy shit" story, our staff, and our website were in place, we were prepared to convert people's interest into action. Even though I'd given a full speech with my fly down, PoP was definitely on its way up.

Mantra 22

———— ✳ ————

FESS UP TO YOUR FAILURES

After spending a month in Laos to work with our team and students on the ground, I returned home to focus on the growing movement behind PoP. We had recently expanded to a third nation, Guatemala, working in the same region around Lake Atitlán where I had lived with Joel Puac years earlier. We had raised over $1 million in 2010 (more than a tenfold increase from the year before), and were setting ambitious goals to break ground on dozens of new schools by the end of the new year. Nobel Peace Prize–winner Archbishop Desmond Tutu even sent us a surprise video to endorse our efforts. I couldn't believe my eyes when I watched him say, "Pencils of Promise . . . keep working, keep learning, the world needs you."

As I saw that video, I thought back to a phrase my friend had scribbled on my apartment whiteboard months earlier: "The most powerful thing in the world is an idea whose time has come." It felt as if this was our moment. The students of Harvard Business

School and Stanford Graduate School of Business, the most discerning business minds of the next generation, had just chosen us as one of the select charities they would fundraise to support. We were hitting on all cylinders.

When a cool opportunity presented itself in the form of the British Airways "Face of Opportunity" contest, I knew I had to submit an entry. Two hundred fifty small-business owners would receive a free flight anywhere in the world. All that was required was an essay or a video on how you would use the flight to advance your organization.

With so much going on, I hadn't had time to work on my application—something I realized one night at 11:40 p.m., twenty minutes before the final entry deadline. With little time, but little to lose, I looked into my iPhone camera and recorded a two-minute video on our work building schools in the developing world and how we would use the flight to bring Lanoy to our headquarters in New York so she could receive an in-depth training from our staff.

The video must have resonated with someone because weeks later we learned that we'd made it into the Top 250 and won a flight. I was elated, and then I was shocked to find out that we'd made it to the Top 10. A weeklong social media voting campaign would determine the top three finalists. Social media? That we could do.

We campaigned hard on Facebook and Twitter, determined to get to the finals to snag the ten free business-class flights that would be awarded to the grand prize–winning organization. I was also eager to garner the publicity for Pencils of Promise that would come along with winning the contest. A few weeks later the ten semifinalists were narrowed down to the final three: a sustainable coffee company called Dunn Bros Coffee, the crowdfunding platform Indiegogo, and us.

I had no idea what to expect in the finals, an event held at Manhattan's giant Marriott Marquis hotel, but it turned out to be a lot more like the TV show *Shark Tank* than the celebratory event I had anticipated. In a room filled with five hundred attendees, I had two minutes to talk about PoP in the "pitch-off." I used what I had learned at Summit Series about making a quick impression and talked about our story, model, and vision to improve the lives of children in poverty by providing access to education. I had given the pitch countless times before—and it had worked in nearly every instance.

But this time when I was finished, the three "celebrity judges," Bill Rancic of *The Apprentice*, Bethenny Frankel of Skinnygirl fame, and real estate mogul Barbara Corcoran from *Shark Tank*, tried to tear me apart. I later learned that they had been instructed to find holes in our companies, although that had never been explained to us before we stepped on the stage.

"How much of the money goes into programs versus overhead?" asked Bill.

"Industry standard would say that any organization that directs over seventy percent toward programs is doing a good job. We try to be as lean as possible, so we've historically put eighty-three to eighty-six percent of funds into programs," I said. The crowd clapped, and Bill nodded his approval.

In between the rapid-fire questions aimed at each finalist, lights flashed and music played loudly; I felt as if I were on a bad reality show. Finally they brought us back together onstage to announce the winner. The first of four votes was the audience favorite, and PoP had received 60 percent of the vote. The second vote was Bill Rancic's, who cast his ballot in our favor. With two out of four total votes, we just needed one more to guarantee we had won. But Bethenny and Barbara both voted for Indiegogo.

"Ladies and gentlemen, for the first time ever, we have a tie!"

boomed the announcer. "We'll now have a live thirty-second pitch-off, and the audience will decide on the winner."

I already won the audience once; I hoped I could do it again. Danae, the cofounder of Indiegogo, went first. She immediately appealed to rationality, touting their proven team and sound business model. Then I was on. I knew I had to tell a story that the audience could connect to emotionally. The crowd was all entrepreneurs. We were driven by the same passion, so I went right to our commonalities. "As anyone with a really big dream who started in a really small room knows, you may have poured your heart and soul into your business, but it was the special people who joined you along the way that made the difference. Those are the people I stand up here representing—the men and women who work in the field, educating our children every day, those are the ones I want to use these flights for. They are the real faces of opportunity."

My thirty seconds were up. The lights started pulsing again, and the clicker votes around the room were counted. This time, I won 85 percent of the audience. Pencils of Promise was announced as the grand-prize winner. Officials from British Airways came out carrying an oversize cardboard check with "10 free business class flights" scribbled in the amount line. Cameras flashed, people I'd never met congratulated me, and interviews commenced. It was an absolute circus, but I was relieved it was over and I couldn't wait to share the news with the team. Ten free flights would be of great value and we had earned a lot of exposure for the organization.

The next afternoon all 250 of the small-business winners were whisked off on a chartered jet to London, where the CEO of British Airways awaited us for a photo opportunity. At the welcome reception, I peeked down at my phone and saw an email from Noah, who was now responsible for our work in Latin America and doing a terrific job. I opened it, and my heart sank.

Appy and I were robbed at knifepoint last night. . . . They stole my
phone and wallet and her BlackBerry and purse. Not sure if we need
to file something with PoP.

The night before had been the Super Bowl, and I knew that
Noah and Appy (our PoP Guatemala Fellow) had gone to a Peace
Corps party in a city several hours away from where we were based
hoping to connect with other NGO workers. I had warned the
staff to be careful in urban areas. And now this had happened.

I assumed Noah had written because he wanted reimbursement
for their stuff. As applause broke out, celebrating PoP's win, and with
little time to focus on this new matter, I dashed an email connecting
Noah to Tom in the New York office so he could help. But I was still
pissed about the whole thing. How could they let this happen?

Although they'd clearly been through a terrible ordeal, it wasn't
PoP's fault that they put themselves in a dangerous situation. Connecting to the emotions of the audience had worked onstage, so I
figured connecting to the emotions of Noah and Appy could bring
about some resolution to this as well. I fired off a reply:

Hey guys,

First off let me say how glad I am that you're both completely okay
and that you weren't hurt at all given what happened recently.

At this point though it's clear that there are some inferences being
made as to whether PoP will be reimbursing you for the items that were
stolen. The truth is that you can make up whatever you want as to what
happened. You can describe it or message it however you want, but I'm
never going to know. What I do know is that we work extremely hard
for every dollar we raise, and that I value every dollar we spend even
more. Also, you guys signed contracts that removed PoP of this liability
and you had your own option to get insurance that would cover you in

case this happened (which Tom can help you follow up on). So as I under-
stand it, the current policy is that PoP shouldn't reimburse anything.

But you are the ones that make our Guatemala programs happen,
you are the ones that took the leap of faith to make PoP your current
life's path. . . . I also hope that you view this organization as your own,
since it truly is the creation of all of us together. Given that, I truly
believe that you guys can make the better call on how PoP should handle
this than I could. Let me know what you think is an ideal outcome for
both PoP and you guys on this, and that's the course we're going to take.
                                                           —Adam

It was not the right response. When I checked my email next,
I found this:

Hey Adam,
I believe we've had a misunderstanding. When I asked if I should
file something with PoP, I was referring to an incident report. I
thought it might be necessary to (1) alert PoP of recent events and (2)
help shape future policy for personnel living abroad. Neither Appy or
I expect any form of reimbursement.
                                                           —Noah

The clarification email was followed by another email, which
was more personal, honest, and appropriately critical of my note.
Noah explained it wasn't a matter of two guys who came up to
them with knives and looted their pockets:

They strangled me, put knives sharply against both of us, threw
Appy up against a wall and wouldn't stop roughing her up until I
was finally able to throw myself on top of her. We weren't just robbed,
we were attacked.

As I continued reading, I couldn't help but think, *This happened because I sent them there*. Noah explained how incredibly disturbing it was to wake up to an email rejecting a request he hadn't made and suggesting dishonesty where there was none: *One would expect that an organization such as PoP, where everyone is sacrificing something to achieve a common goal, would be more supportive of its staff*. As for Appy, he said she was already quite rattled by the incident, but was even further disturbed by the way I handled it and was now thinking about leaving the organization.

One of my closest friends and best leaders was taken aback by something I did, and one of our best people was thinking about quitting. Noah and Appy had gone through something traumatic, and it happened under my leadership. To that point everything had been so positive. We were building schools and changing the world. Nothing worse than my motorbike accident had occurred. Now, two people had had their lives threatened working on our vision.

I never thought starting PoP could lead to someone's life being truly endangered, but suddenly I saw that as a real possibility. Failing to immediately recognize the seriousness of what could have happened made me see my flaws as a leader. I had to acknowledge that we were no longer just kids traveling the world and helping people; real risks were associated with our work.

I had wrongly responded as a CEO by addressing financial concerns without truly focusing on my employees' well-being. I was trying to protect the organization, but in doing so I neglected the very people who *were* the organization. It was a massive failure. I had alienated two of our best people. They'd wanted compassion and I'd focused on covering costs.

Leadership isn't just about telling people what to do. It's about doing the right thing even when it's not written in the rulebook. The first thing I did was to tell them how sorry I was for my behavior. I had to own it fully. We all make mistakes; it's the weak who make excuses too.

But my work would have to go beyond patching things up with Appy and Noah. The incident highlighted just how little we'd prepared for those types of incidents. We immediately established organization-wide contingency plans to help us prepare for, and when necessary deal with, the unexpected. We created a policy and guidelines handbook specifically for international staff to complement the general one we had for all staff. We began taking certain precautions before team members could go in-country (obtaining insurance, registering phone numbers with the national phone company, signing vehicle waiver documents, etc.). We codified a list of best practices for in-country staff and built an incident report form so that we could track, address, and reduce future occurrences. A rule was even put in place that mandated a Skype call within forty-eight hours of any emergency so that it would be resolved via face-to-face communication rather than email.

From my awful mishandling of that one situation, we emerged a stronger whole. PoP seemed to mature by several years almost overnight. By recognizing the deficiencies we were previously unable to see, we tightened up every area across the organization and our team became closer than ever. Errors force you to pause, evaluate, and iterate. As much as we dread them, they are veiled blessings that turn mirrors of reflection into windows of insight.

I personally learned that failure is a necessary step toward achievement. In fact, it often accelerates it. The British Airways contest gave me confidence that we were on the right track, yet it took an international stumble to demonstrate that the biggest opportunities for growth are not found in the midst of success, but in the methods through which we address failure.

LEARN TO CLOSE THE LOOP

Now in our own space, blaring music, learning over lunch, we started to focus even more on our company culture. While traveling back and forth to visit our schools, I thought a lot about what kind of organization we wanted to become. I wanted people to love working at PoP. To succeed in this work, which none of us had ever before done, we needed fierce commitment. But how could we inspire that?

I defined five key elements that our culture had to exude to draw and retain top talent: happiness, friendship, reward, improvement, and fun. I tried to come up with ways to deliver on those values, so we added practices like a monthly meditation, with the whole team sitting in silence for fifteen minutes and focusing on being in the present. We also started a "daily jukebox," wherein every day one person would pick a song to listen to and we'd all stop during lunch to hear the story behind the selection before absorbing the beats. It was not only a blast, it brought the team together as friends and individuals. We couldn't compensate people well financially, but we could provide them with fulfillment and passion.

Music and meditation aside, what really brought us joy was working for something beyond ourselves. We recognized that we weren't working alone, and the people who helped us along the way made everything feel deeper and more connected. When I looked at social media, people gained engaged Twitter followers not just by broadcasting their own accomplishments, but by replying to the tweets of others so they furthered the conversation. Being inclusive was an effective approach—and it felt a lot better too. As we grew, our internal culture focused more and more on the celebration of others, especially through connecting individuals to our work on the ground.

In an effort to become better at acknowledging the people who helped us make an impact, I mandated a handwritten thank-you note policy. Everyone had to write two thank-you notes a month, one personal and one professional. Twice a month, at noon, we would stop whatever we were working on, distribute Pencils of Promise stationery (having forgone this before, we ordered it now specifically for this reason), and give everyone fifteen minutes to write a letter, address an envelope, and seal it. We collected them, added postage, and put them in the mail.

I had been remiss on writing thank-you notes myself and was two years behind on one letter in particular. When Pencils of Promise was only six months old and completing its first school, I received a check from someone I'd never met—and someone I'd never thanked. We referred to the communication that explained to someone where his or her money went as "closing the loop." And while many organizations were simply content to take a donor's money and mail out a receipt at year's end, it became paramount within PoP to "close the loop" by showing people the change they'd created in the lives of others by sending them the exact GPS location of their school along with photos, videos, and stories from the ground.

My friend Claire had helped us plan one of our early events to fundraise for our first school. I had snapped pictures of our progress with the build—bricks being laid, surrounded by bamboo scaffolding, and emailed them to the forty people who had been so helpful in getting the school off the ground. In one photo, the building looked like a skeleton, but it was still amazing to me, and I hoped others would feel the same way.

I soon received an email back from Claire:

As you may know, I currently work at a construction company. I forwarded your email to my boss because I know he is interested in international development. 20 minutes later he came to my desk with a check to Pencils of Promise in the amount of $1,000. I can't believe it. I thought you'd want to know!

What? I thought I read it wrong. No one outside of close friends had ever given us a donation that reached $100, and here we got $1,000 from someone we didn't know? I forwarded the email to Mimi and the others. We were all in awe.

Now, more than two years later, I thought back to the massive impact this stranger had on our organization. He believed in us far before anyone else had, and I had to let him know how grateful I was for his early support.

I emailed Claire, who was now living in London, and asked her for her boss's name and address. It was long overdue, but she sent me his name, Larry Petretti, and I wrote him a heartfelt note:

You don't know me, but two years ago you took a leap of faith to support Pencils of Promise. You gave us $1,000 and the confidence to keep working on a big dream. You were the first major donor we had and helped build one of the first Pencils of Promise schools. Now we've opened up more than fifteen schools and have plans to break ground on our 50th before the end of the year. I'll never be able to properly articulate how much you changed my life, but I hope the enclosed picture demonstrates how much you've changed someone else's life as well. Best wishes, Adam Braun.

On recent visits I'd been leaving colored pencils and hundreds of sheets of paper with the teachers in our schools. When I'd return to that village several days later, the students would hand me hundreds of drawings, which I then mailed to supporters. I included one of these hand-drawn pictures in the note to Larry and placed a Post-it on it explaining its origin.

Soon, I got an email back:

Dear Adam,

Thank you for your wonderful letter. I feel humbled that I could have made such an impact on your organization. I love what you have done. I have been involved with fundraising for more charities than I can remember and your organization is just so pure, so grassroots. You are making such a difference in a place and with people that would never have a chance otherwise. Education is the greatest gift one can give. It makes you realize how simple it would be to solve so many problems that plague our world if we could just focus on educating the masses instead of building bigger tanks and warplanes.

I pray that you continue your good work and keep me posted on your progress.

Kind regards,
Larry

Larry and I corresponded some more and I invited him to the office to meet in person and speak as part of our Lunch and Learn series. I actually started the program as a way to spend my days more efficiently by getting people to come to me rather than going to them. Esteemed people with significant authority usually expect you to come to their office, but by inviting those same people to "speak to our staff at a Lunch and Learn," they often felt honored to be asked to more than just a standard meeting and usually made the trek to our little Lower East Side office.

Not only was I able to double the number of meetings I could take in a day by never leaving the office, but the team got so much out of it too. After sharing his or her own story, we'd then have each speaker ask one question that every staff member answered aloud. Heads of marketing agencies asked questions like "What's your favorite font?" and "If you were a brand, who would you be?" while nonprofit CEOs asked, "What inspired you to join Pencils of Promise?" and "Why are you passionate about education in particular?"

These group discussions created a profound connection between the speakers and our team, while also enabling our young staff to hone their public-speaking skills. This practice became such an important part of our culture that we would even require candidates we were interviewing to participate.

I was pretty surprised one afternoon when Larry, whom I had imagined as a burly guy running a construction company, showed up in a pin-striped power suit. The rest of us, in T-shirts and sneakers, packed into the main room to meet our first major donor and hear what wisdom he had to impart to us. Larry told us his story of building his company from nothing to now doing all subcontracting work for the build-out of the offices for IBM and Bank of America. When we got to the question segment, I was blown away because his question was so different from any that we had heard before. "How can I help each of you best accomplish your goals with Pencils of Promise?" he asked with sincerity. All twenty people in the room took their time thoughtfully answering the question. When it was my turn, I looked around the crammed space and said the first thing that came to mind.

"If we ever get a new office, you can help us find a good architect," I joked.

"I'll do better," he said. "I'll find you an architect and then have my subcontractors build out the entire thing for free."

With that promise, as we were squeezed together in a small room, I knew we wouldn't be there for long. What really knit us together—a commitment to improving ourselves and the world—was going to keep us just as tightly bound. A simple handwritten thank-you letter facilitated our getting our future office built for free, saving hundreds of thousands of dollars.

Later that month, I received a frantic email from Brad. *You're not going to believe this, but the CEO of Saatchi & Saatchi (the largest advertising agency in the world) wrote his daily blog post about Pencils of Promise. People in the advertising industry are blowing up my email about it!* Brad sent me a link, and when I clicked into the blog of Kevin Roberts, I read his impassioned post about the merits of our work and approach. The power of simply following up, or "closing the loop," was so evident from the experience with Larry, I decided I had to use this as an opportunity to reach out.

I searched online for any way to get in touch with him and finally was able to get a note through. I got an email back from his assistant, with a PDF of my email printed out and Kevin's response written by hand on the right side of the paper.

Adam, good to hear from you. I'm on the road for the next few weeks and not really in NY much at all I'm afraid. My assistant will set up a call when I'm back. . . . I'd love to hear your plans. Best, KR

The call itself was a whirlwind. Kevin didn't waste any time or words. He was a model of passion and efficiency. I frantically tried to scribble down notes during our thirty-minute chat, but the pen could barely keep up with all of his brilliant insights and advice. As our time came to a close, I asked him if we could speak again in the near future. His response was quick and dead serious: "We'll speak again when you reach your hundredth school."

I almost laughed out loud. We were two and a half years in and had built a little more than twenty-five schools. I believed that we would get there many years into the future, but I'd never even considered that we would reach a hundred schools anytime soon. But perhaps it wasn't all that unrealistic? I think he heard my hesitation on the other end of the line, and he offered a final few words of assurance: "Here's my best advice: make the little decisions with your head and the big ones with your heart. Do that, and you'll be just fine."

He was right. Kevin had illuminated a Big Hairy Audacious Goal (BHAG) to drive toward, and if I stuck to my gut, we might get there. I'd never considered it before the call, but I decided to set our sights on building our hundredth school by the end of the following year. Relentlessly following up on every lead had paid off. PoP was built on the underdog mentality, so only a goal that big would seem right to motivate the hell out of us and serve as our rallying cry over the next twenty months.

CHANGE YOUR WORDS
TO CHANGE YOUR WORTH

On a warm summer evening, I found myself on a stunning rooftop terrace in midtown Manhattan, attending a launch party for a large media company. Partygoers in expensive suits and tight cocktail dresses milled about, sipping fine champagne and admiring the city skyline. The Empire State Building was just a few blocks away, towering over us in a reddish glow. Prominent venture capitalists, journalists, investors, and business executives mingled, exchanging summer plans and their latest business ideas. Although I'd just returned from a trip to Guatemala where I'd spent my days with children more interested in markers than markets, the conversations that night were enlightening, and I didn't feel all that dissimilar to most people in attendance.

I began talking with a guy in his midforties who ran an investment fund and told me about his latest capital raise. We hit it off while discussing the differences between start-ups on the East and

West Coasts, and I enjoyed learning about how he evaluated new investment opportunities. Although I'd left that space a while ago, I still knew it well enough to carry a solid conversation and felt as if we were speaking the same language. Then he asked what I did.

"I run a nonprofit organization called Pencils of Promise."

"Oh," he replied, somewhat taken aback. "And you do that full-time?"

More than full-time, I thought, feeling a bit judged. "Yeah, I do. I used to work at Bain, but left to work on the organization full-time."

"Wow, good for you," he said in the same tone you'd use to address a small child, then immediately looked over my shoulder for someone new to approach. He soon waved at someone across the terrace and feigned interest in me with one last question:

"Tell me the name of your project again?"

Project? It wasn't the first time someone had referred to PoP with that dismissive term. "Pencils of Promise," I said. He then gave me his card, another way of saying, *This conversation is now over*, and walked away.

In the awkward and electrically charged pause that followed, I couldn't help but feel less than equal. Worse, the feeling was becoming all too familiar.

On my subway ride home that night I began to reflect on the many times that this scenario had happened since I'd started Pencils of Promise. Conversations began on an equal footing, but the word *nonprofit* could stop a discussion in its tracks and strip our work of its value and true meaning. That one word could shift the conversational dynamic so that the other person was suddenly speaking down to me. As mad as I was at this guy, it suddenly hit me. I was to blame for his lackluster response. With one word, *nonprofit*, I had described my company as something that stood in stark opposition to the one metric that his company was being most evaluated by. I had used a negative word, *non*, to detail our work when that inaccurately described what we did. Our primary driver was not the avoidance of profits, but the abundance of social impact.

Non is defined as "of little or no consequence: unimportant: worthless." Worthless? Clearly, something needed to change. Why were we the only industry that introduced itself with a negative when we existed not to reduce profits, but to foster a profusion of purpose? Instead of introducing ourselves by touting what we didn't do, shouldn't we share what we did do? Shouldn't we boldly proclaim that we work to produce social good in the largest measurable form possible? It was time to remove the stigma that vastly separates nonprofits from their for-profit counterparts. Even though PoP would always remain a 501(c)(3), not-for-profit organization, couldn't we at least adopt the mind-set of a for-profit company that focused on structure, results, and adherence to long-term strategic impact?

As I started to think about it more, I realized that I'd never once considered myself a "nonprofit person." I thought of myself as a business-driven entrepreneur who wanted to work on global education. No part of me wanted to be poor; I just refused to let the size of my bank account serve as the yardstick of my success. While I once thought the best measure of accomplishment was monetary wealth, my path over the past few years had shown me that real value comes from investing in the well-being of others. I wanted to spend my time maximizing purpose rather than profit, which seemed to be a common characteristic of many of the people I now looked up to. We adhered to a different bottom line, but that didn't stop us from wanting to see that final number become as big as possible, whether it stood for children educated or lives improved.

That night I decided to start using a new phrase that more appropriately labeled the motivation behind our work. By changing the words you use to describe something, you can change how others perceive it. For too long we had allowed society to judge us with shackling expectations that weren't supportive of scale. I knew that the only way to win the respect of our for-profit peers would be to wed our values and idealism to business acumen. Rather than thinking of ourselves as *nonprofit*, we would begin to refer to our work as *for-purpose*.

Although this was just a simple twist in language, the internal impact on our organization was profound. When we started to pull apart our model, we noticed some real issues. Great businesses make it quick and simple to buy their product, but we were still fixated on explaining every detail of every school to every potential donor. The first thing we needed to improve was the accessibility of our work. As soon as we broke down our numbers and streamlined communications to show that it only cost $25 to educate one child, $10,000 to build a classroom, and $25,000 to build a full school, people got it right away and understood the difference they could make. Conversations became more direct, and we could tell within minutes at what level someone might be interested in getting involved.

We also noticed that many people didn't trust charities because they didn't know what their money was going toward (programs, office rent, salaries, or something else?). Thus, our second focus became to differentiate ourselves by becoming totally transparent and building trust. We decided to hold an annual gala to cover our operating expenses and then promised to commit 100 percent of funds donated online throughout the year to our school programs. Every penny raised on our website now goes directly to support our students and teachers. We even started letting donors who funded full schools decide in which country their school would be built, and we offered to take them into the field so they could see their school open firsthand. I started hosting weekly webinars to which anyone could sign in and ask me questions. We made our financials easy to find rather than buried within our website. One of our founding values was "Donors should have the ability to choose where their money goes," so we decided to allow anyone to allocate 100 percent of their funds directly into the exact areas of our work that they'd like to support. People found our openness refreshing, and that cultivated a sense of trust.

Third, we decided to treat our work like a business, not a charity. We had to set clear goals and then hold ourselves accountable. As strange as it sounds, this meant that we had to start firing volunteers who didn't deliver. For years we had people that worked on PoP part-time and full-time whom we would never let go because of the generosity of their service. But over time I noticed that certain people became energy vampires, sucking time and enthusiasm out of others without providing value in return. At first it seemed laughable to consider firing someone who wasn't even being paid and who dedicated thirty hours per week to our cause, but removing people who didn't produce became imperative to setting an expectation of excellent performance across the entire team.

We had built a culture of good intentions and boundless passion, but when it came to measuring our impact in the field, that was not enough. We needed to introduce another kind of structure. We decided that we would govern ourselves with the same ruthless commitment to results as the world's best Fortune 500 companies. We started spending less time focusing on how good we felt and much more energy measuring the positive impact we could create with every dollar. We started to study the metrics, and we figured out exactly what it would take to reach our hundredth school by the end of the following year. With a roadmap in place, the goal started to feel attainable, and while we marched toward it, we also objectively measured whether our programs were succeeding in the places where we'd already established schools. Photos of smiling children were good, but hard data proving that we'd increased literacy and math skills were even better.

Fourth, we had to change how we worked with the members of our PoP ecosystem. Every person we interacted with, from the parent of a student to the CEO of a corporate sponsor, had to see himself or herself as a partner in our mission rather than someone giving or receiving a handout. We purposely didn't provide the entire funding for any of our school builds because we wanted to work with people who had a hand up, ready to participate, not those who simply had a hand out. We decided that every community had to provide 10 to 20 percent of the funding before we'd break ground on a school. Because the majority of families where we operated lived on $1 to $2 per day and spare cash was rare, most of these contributions were made by helping to physically build the school (clearing land, digging the foundation, or laying bricks) and by providing raw materials such as wood, gravel, and sand. This meant thousands of parents investing in their children's educations and hundreds of new local jobs being created on school sites.

Lastly, we changed the way we approached our work with companies and their sponsorships. We started to put a price tag on our ability to help start-ups and established brands market themselves while also building their internal morale. Employees felt stronger about their work when they knew that they were contributing to the betterment of society, which was something we could beautifully and tangibly make happen through integrated partnerships. When our Schools4All campaign with Justin raised $300,000 in ten weeks by signing up more than thirty thousand young fundraisers, companies really started to see that we could help them reach their target audiences too.

For the first time we started saying no to certain offered partnerships, to ensure that we didn't dilute our own brand. We invested our efforts into fewer but larger collaborations. Through this approach, we ultimately landed partnerships with Google, Microsoft, Delta, Warby Parker, and many other best-in-class companies. They still viewed their donations as charitable contributions, but they also saw a return on their investment by having an active marketing partner to help promote their philanthropic efforts. Whether it was through cobranded events or receiving a portion of their sales, we could introduce their product to a new audience while enabling their employees to feel connected to a cause. By taking this approach, the amount of money we received from corporate sponsors doubled that year. We decided to use that money to match potential contributions from individual donors (giving us the ability to announce statements like, "Your donations this week up to $10,000 will be matched by our friends at Barnes & Noble"). Personal donations increased while companies benefited from the positive exposure. It was a complete win-win, and it exemplified how we could earn money rather than beg for it.

Later that summer I dug up the business card of the investor from the rooftop and invited him to lunch. I wanted to tell him that he'd helped me change the language I used to describe my work. Chatting over a soup and a sandwich in TriBeCa, I shared my newly developed belief that any company that treats its social mission as its true bottom line should call itself a for-purpose. He smiled, nodded, and said, "I like that line of thinking."

Several weeks later, I received an envelope in the mail; in it was a check from this gentleman to help build one of our new schools in Guatemala. He now saw his contribution as an investment. He wasn't increasing his annual profits, but he definitely saw a spike in his sense of purpose.

A GOAL REALIZED
IS A GOAL DEFINED

It hardly happened overnight, but with lots of practice and experience, I began to feel more comfortable speaking in public. Actually, I began to enjoy it. When I received an invitation from Semester at Sea to go back on the ship as a guest lecturer, I jumped at the opportunity. I would join the voyage in Morocco, spend a full week with the students as the ship traveled along the African coastline, then disembark in Ghana, where I would travel independently. The organizers even sweetened the deal by letting me bring a guest, which was great because I didn't know a single other person on board.

I invited my mother to celebrate her fifty-fifth birthday.

Once I set foot on the MV *Explorer*, I was overcome by nostalgia. The fresh smell of my cabin's interior immediately brought me back to that feeling of being a student on the ship six years earlier. This was the experience that had most shaped the person I'd become deep down inside. Time seemed to accordion—I simultaneously felt so far removed from those days and yet I could envision myself right back in my old Nike Air Force 1s.

Most of my recent speeches had been at corporate conferences, so this would be the first time in a while that I was speaking to college students. It felt freeing: I didn't have to sugarcoat anything; I could simply speak from the heart.

When it came time for my first talk, I focused on what I thought the students would most want to hear. Many of them had told me that this was their first time traveling independently, so I shared some advice on Backpacking 101.

Reflecting on my experiences in Latin America, I advised, "First, accept that plans change and new opportunities will suddenly present themselves while traveling, so just go with the flow. If you remove your cynicism and allow yourself to be astonished by the wonders of the world, you'll be blown away by the memories you'll make via the unexpected itinerary. Second, if you make yourself a target, you'll become one. Don't wear bright clothing, and if you don't want someone touching your valued possessions, keep them in a money belt down your pants. Your privates should stay next to your privates. Trust me, no one will be going there without your permission. Third, music and body language are universally spoken, so when someone invites you to dance, let go of your inhibitions and dance. And lastly, when in doubt, just say you're Canadian. People hate a lot of countries, but no one hates the Canadians."

A handful of kids laughed, and I could tell the three hundred students in the room appreciated the honest and relatable advice. I knew that because this talk was the first time that I used a technique called "one person, one thought."

Weak speakers look down at the floor, good speakers look up

but scan the room, great speakers make eye contact selectively, and exceptional speakers deliver every complete thought directly to one person in the audience, making that person feel like the center of the room—and then they move on and do it again. We've all been in that position when a speaker looks right at you, and for a few fleeting moments your heart starts to race. You are locked in.

I started to look directly at just one student for the entirety of every thought I delivered and attempted to tell them a story as if no one else was listening. It emboldened me to speak with greater conviction, and as the speech gained momentum, I could feel the pulse of the room elevate. After nearly an hour of talking about what I knew and loved, I ended with the most sincere beliefs that I could share.

"You have to find a mantra and live it fully. The one I'd adopt right now if I were you is something I found on the inside of a friend's journal last year: 'You may be safe, but I am free.' Take advantage of the freedom that comes with your youth. Inhale life, exhale fire, and embrace the late, sleepless nights, because that's when the magic happens—when everyone else is asleep and you're awake thinking about the world as it is, and the world as it could be. Make the most of those moments," I said forcefully. "And in the coming years people will tell you that you're too young to change the world. I'm here to tell you, that's fucking bullshit."

I'd never cursed in a speech before. It just came out. An audible gasp filled the room. There was dead silence. Then, much to my surprise, the students began clapping raucously with agreement. After months and months of practiced pitches back home, it felt good to simply speak the truth unfiltered. That night, I vowed, going forward, to speak from the heart no matter which audience I was addressing.

*   *   *

Following an invigorating week on the ship, I felt like a new man. The students' sense of wonder and willingness to sprint toward the unknown was refreshing. After my second lecture fifty students even stuck around to brainstorm about a campaign we would launch the following year called the Impossible Ones, which would celebrate the spirit these students embodied by having people take on "impossible" challenges to raise money for PoP. I stepped off the MV *Explorer* in Accra, Ghana, ready to explore the country as a potential location for PoP's expansion into Africa.

After a year of research, Ghana was our top choice due to its tremendous need for primary education in the countryside. Since we would need to find a local partner to help us get a foot in the door before building our own fully independent operations (this usually takes about a year), our team set up several visits for me with local NGOs.

On the three-hour shuttle ride to Ho, the capital of the deeply impoverished Volta Region, the poverty juxtaposed with the beauty of this West African nation was captivating. Towering waterfalls dropped misted waters like snowfall onto the mountainsides, while malnourished children emerged from mud huts to wave at each passing car. When we arrived in the dusty capital, I was greeted by the founding team from Disaster Volunteers of Ghana (DIVOG), an NGO started by four Ghanaian friends, which had been building schools in the region for years. Right away, they briefed me on statistics that demonstrated the need for trained teachers and new classrooms throughout Volta.

The following morning, they took me in an old van to see some of their project sites. In one village after another, I saw school-less sites and met children without classrooms or any opportunity to learn. In those same communities, parents verbally committed to provide 100 percent of the labor to build their children's school if they received funding for the raw materials and a commitment from the education ministry to provide trained teachers. The culture was one of complete community participation. In the days ahead I spent hours with members of the education ministry, who agreed to provide trained teachers for any school we built, and I visited several schools under construction where I witnessed that 100 percent labor commitment being fulfilled. The determination of the Ghanaian people won me over—as did a boy named Justice.

Two years earlier I had received an email from a Ghanaian student named Justice, who told me of his dream to bring education to the children of his country, who were learning under mango trees instead of in classrooms and often had no teachers or books at all. He had discovered PoP through Facebook, and his email was so uplifting that we started corresponding regularly and eventually talked on Skype too. Back then PoP was just getting started, but when the Semester at Sea voyage brought me to Ghana, I knew I had to find him.

On my last day in Ho, I finally got to meet Justice in person. We spent the entire day together, walking through monkey forests and remote villages. Before I left, he asked me for one thing:

"When you go back home, you will not forget about us?"

"Of course I won't forget about you," I said.

"Then you must promise me that you will come back. And Pencils of Promise will work in Ghana to support the education of our children."

"I hope so." I meant it.

"Hope is not enough. You have to believe, and then it will be so."

When I went back to my hotel that night, I wrote an email to our team stating that I expected us to expand to Ghana the following year. Rainer Maria Rilke said, "Live not in dreams, but in contemplation of a reality that is perhaps the future." It was time to make that future happen. We'd need to raise a lot of money at our upcoming gala to make it possible, but the first step was acknowledging the goal itself.

Six weeks later, Justice's voice was still ringing in my head on the biggest night in the history of the organization, the night of our first gala. We had thrown large events before, but this was a long way from my twenty-fifth birthday party where people launched PoP with $20 and $25 donations. Gala tickets were now $500, and purchasing a table cost $10,000 to $50,000. I was amazed when we sold out three weeks in advance and there was a fifty-person wait-list of generous supporters willing to pay $1,000 each the night of the event—all of whom we had to reluctantly turn away because we were so over capacity.

I had never attended a major gala, and now I was leading this one, attended by Shaquille O'Neal and Usher. One of the evening's honorees was Justin Bieber, who was by then donating $1 from every US concert ticket to PoP. We were also honoring my brother, Scooter, for his tremendous advocacy and support of our work, along with Rich Lent and the entire AgencyNet team. Sophia Bush, the beautiful actress and activist, was the night's host.

I had invested so many hours in getting this night right, and I knew that my opening speech would set the tone for the entire evening. As the program began, I made my way toward the stage and, with the audience of 550 people, watched a short video of our work. On the screen flashed the words I had spoken in tiny rooms so many times before: "We don't just want you to support us, we want you to join us." After speaking passionately about how much she believed in our work, Sophia, whom I had met through Summit Series, invited me onto the stage.

As I stepped up to the podium, I took a long, deep breath. The confidence I'd gained on Semester at Sea led me to believe that I could wing anything, but it suddenly hit me that I'd only have one shot at this. I scanned the audience and saw my entire family. My parents. My siblings. My grandmothers. My cousins. My friends. My team. I looked into each of their eyes and felt the heat in my hands start to dissipate. *One person, one thought*, I told myself.

I began by telling the story of the boy who asked for the single pencil, then projected an image of the $25 that started the organization. Each of these set the context, but the next image was something I'd never before shown anyone. The large screen projected a handwritten page from my leatherbound journal. After a decade of writing in these journals, filling hundreds of pages, I read an entire page aloud for the first time. It described the night that the name Pencils of Promise entered my mind at the Philharmonic and the moment when the idea for the organization was born.

Sometimes you just know. With absolute conviction. The complete absence of doubt is so rare it generates a sense of excitement that's so powerful it becomes shocking. . . . That name just appeared in my head, and I remember a hard closing of my eyes followed by an opening and a quick punch of breath. It literally knocked the wind out of me, left me searching for air, a tingling of excitement surging through my chest. Yes. With absolute conviction. Everything had changed.

People began to nod their heads and clap. They felt what I felt, that we were participating in something bigger than any one of us as individuals, and that we had the opportunity to do something remarkable together. I then showed the video of Nith and Nuth, so that every person in the room could connect with the children we were working to support. The groundwork had been laid, now we just had to follow through.

Lanoy had flown in days earlier and received a standing ovation when introduced. She and Leslie tied baci string around each of the honorees' wrists when they took the stage, and Justin, Scooter, and Rich all gave moving speeches. Their conviction in our work set up a perfect opportunity to go big, and just before the part of the night when the auctioneer would encourage major pledges from those in attendance, I shared one more announcement. The SAS experience had given me the confidence to speak our loftiest aspirations aloud, and this one night was the only chance we'd get to fulfill Justice's request. I needed to announce a clear goal, and the transformational outcome it would produce if we hit it. Defining both cleanly was the key.

"Since PoP was founded, we've wanted to work on the African continent. If we raise one million dollars tonight, we will expand into Ghana next year. You can make that happen. That's not just an idea, it's a promise."

Hands started to go up with pledges, and the room willed itself forward.

By the time the event ended, we had done it. We'd raised over $1 million. In doing so we received several major five-figure and six-figure pledges, proving that our work appealed to philanthropists of all levels. But the night wasn't just about the money. It was the culmination of everything that we had been through as an organization. The validation of everything we'd worked toward. All of the late nights and individual meetings, the thousands of tiny wins, enabled this one big night to come together perfectly.

After all of the attendees left, only my family and our staff remained. The adage says to keep your friends close and your enemies closer; I believe in keeping your friends close and your family even closer. We begged the band to keep playing, and everyone danced together, hugging with euphoria. We looked so different on the outside, yet each of us shared a common thread. It wasn't just the baci strings around our wrists, but the knowledge that this one night had put PoP on a whole new level. We were headed to Africa, and there was no turning back.

SURROUND YOURSELF WITH THOSE WHO MAKE YOU BETTER

Although the achievements of Pencils of Promise may have been rising, I also wanted something else—to find someone to love—and in that pursuit, I was getting nowhere. I saw how special my parents' relationship was and wanted a lifelong partner just as they had, but finding the right person was proving difficult.

For as long as I could remember, I had been telling my mom that my future wife would have a cool name and green eyes. I've never known why I had that premonition, but I'd had this intuitive sense of the person I'd marry throughout my entire life. Each time someone tried to set me up with a girl, the first question I'd ask was "What's her name?"—hoping that it sounded unique. I dated plenty of girls in New York, many of whom I genuinely liked, but I didn't fall head over heels in love with any of them.

My deepest relationship was with Pencils of Promise, and I hadn't connected with anyone on a level that compared. Being alone started to frustrate me. When I would think about the type of girl I was looking for, the qualities were so specific yet contradictory: someone who laughed a lot but knew how to hold a serious debate; a girl who could backpack and stay on mud floors in bamboo huts, but could also walk the red carpet at a gala; a person who was close with her family but willing to go off the grid for a while. Friends would throw their hands in the air and wish me luck. Eventually Hoolie described this mythical girl accurately. "You're looking for a unicorn," he joked. "She sounds amazing, but I'm not sure she exists."

On a blazing-orange summer night, I found myself chatting at a rooftop barbecue with my friend Dan's girlfriend, Laura. Our PoP events had brought together many new couples, this pair being one of them, and I joked with Laura about finding me a match among her friends. When Dan peered over her shoulder to ask what we were discussing, she mentioned that we were talking about a girl for me. "Who, Tehillah?" Dan asked innocently. Laura replied, "No, she lives too far away. I was thinking of someone else."

But that name alone set off something inside me. I had never heard such a beautiful name in my entire life. I had to know more.

"Wait, who is Tehillah?" I asked.

"Oh, she's my best friend from high school. She's the most down-to-earth person I know, and Jewish too."

"Where's she from?" I pressed.

"Well, she's originally from South Africa. But she moved to Boston when she was nine and stayed there after college to model."

"And she's actually Jewish? That's a huge deal in my family," I said.

"Oh, yeah. Her dad is a rabbi. Her name means 'praise' in Hebrew."

"So you're telling me your best friend is a South African beauty named Tehillah, whose father is a rabbi, and she's down-to-earth too? I only have one more question." I took a deep breath. "What color are her eyes?"

Laura paused, picturing her. "They're green."

My heart exploded. I had to meet her. "You have to give me her number. I want to invite her down to the city. I need to meet this girl," I said urgently.

"Don't you want to see her picture?" Laura asked.

"Nope. Photos create false expectations. I just want to meet her in person and see if there's a mutual attraction. But I have a really good feeling about this."

"Okay, we'll make it happen," Laura said, and a week later sent over a phone number for me to call, letting me know that Tehillah was interested in meeting too.

I must have written and rewritten that first text message thirty times. I wasn't sure whether I should try to be funny or polite, respectful or forward. One of my friends consistently won over girls through his over-the-top-but-with-a-wink approach. He'd send messages like *Are you ready for the most dangerous date of your life?* and *I'm bringing a parachute and a kayak to the bar. What are you bringing?* Girls found him hysterical, so I decided to take his approach.

Hi, it's Adam, Laura and Dan's friend. I hear you're coming to NYC and down to get drinks with a charming stranger? I typed out. I thought, *Please don't screw this up,* and pressed send.

Minutes later, I got a reply: *Oh, we'll see how charming you are. I heard you're terrible. I hear you rob banks and are wanted in nine different states.* She was witty! I laughed out loud while walking to the subway, and the text message banter began. Messages flew back and forth, each revealing a bit more about our personalities and pasts. By the time we finally met in person several weeks later, seated across from each other at Dan's birthday dinner, I had already told everyone I knew about this mystery girl. Fortunately, she was everything I had hoped and much more.

The first thing I noticed about Tehillah was her warmth. She made every single person she spoke with feel as if he or she were the center of the world. Her beauty was beyond description. Blond hair, tan skin, and emerald eyes that stared right through me. Although I was horrifically awkward for the first fifteen minutes, stumbling over my words, we found comfort in each other's presence throughout the night. I had never believed in love at first sight, but I was experiencing it. We danced, laughed, and even shared a first kiss.

I was completely smitten. The next morning I emailed my entire family to tell them that I had met the girl I would one day marry. Just as my dad had done, I even wrote it on a piece of paper and placed the message in a bottle to be revealed on our wedding day. I had found someone to share my life's journey with. Her name was Tehillah, and she was a unicorn with green eyes.

Having Tehillah as my partner changed my perspective on nearly everything. She helped me put my phone away at the end of the day, taught me to eat better and exercise more often. When I would blab on and on about PoP, she would remind me that no one likes someone who is one-dimensional and that every person I encountered that day was fighting an important battle too. Most important, she made me want to be a better listener, not just a better speaker.

Because I was so excited about how well things were going with her, I found myself bringing her up during meetings with potential donors, and much to my surprise it created a whole new layer of connection. People can read each other's bio on the Internet, but getting to know who someone is goes a lot deeper than what their job title tells you. By openly speaking about falling in love, I got into conversations about people's families, how they met their husbands and wives, and what mattered most in their lives. These discussions weren't about our work, but they created a bond that felt authentic rather than transactional.

This was exactly what led me to connect with one of the most inspiring people I have ever met, and one of the people who played a transformative role in the evolution of PoP.

I had heard Ray Chambers, the legendary financier and philanthropist, speak at the Google Zeitgeist conference in Arizona. I was motivated by the success he'd achieved in private equity and how he also used his passion and power to solve some of the world's biggest problems through cofounding high-impact organizations such as America's Promise, Points of Light, and Malaria No More. Ray was the ultimate example of what I hoped to one day achieve.

Around this time we were looking to bolster the PoP board of directors with one well-known individual who would add visibility and tremendous credibility to our work. Ray Chambers was the embodiment of that, but he was so many leagues ahead. I didn't think I'd ever meet him without a podium or stage separating us. But remarkably, we were introduced via email and suddenly had an hour-long one-on-one meeting scheduled at his office.

Ray had been appointed by the United Nations secretary-general as the first UN Special Envoy for Malaria, and based on how effective he'd been in that position, he'd been elevated to serve as the special envoy in charge of holding the world's leaders accountable to each of the health-related Millennium Development Goals. After passing by the UN emblem on the front door of his Manhattan office, I was ushered into a stunning conference room overlooking Central Park.

Within a few minutes, Ray entered. His gray hair was neatly combed, and his pinstripe suit seemed fitting for someone of such esteemed authority. He invited me to sit on one of the two plush brown leather sofas and began to speak in his distinctive, breathy tone. "So, Adam, it sounds like you are doing wonderful things with P.O.P.," he said with a smile.

I knew Ray was a former private equity guy, and although I planned to detail my finance background and hoped we'd connect on our shared paths combining business with philanthropy, I didn't open with that. He'd allotted a full hour for us together, so I began with my personal story. I told him about the ship and the Wave. I told him about my experience with certain death, and how it led me to finding my sense of purpose.

Then I introduced our unique approach to increasing educational opportunity in the developing world. I used every business term in the book, talking about the efficiencies we were trying to leverage and the operational model we aimed to scale and replicate. I figured the opening story would give him context, but that the businesslike approach would be what he cared about most.

When I finally stopped talking, Ray closed his eyes and leaned his head back. I was waiting for him to give a detailed critique of our model. Instead, he responded, "Well, Adam, what you are describing—what you have experienced—is something that sages have sought for thousands of years. It is what the Dalai Lama teaches. What you are describing is the state of bliss. Bliss does not come from materials or possessions, it comes from fulfilling one's purpose in this existence."

For the next ten minutes, Ray only spoke about achieving bliss through service to others. I was astounded. He spoke every word with such sincerity. I could hear Tehillah's advice not to be so one-dimensional ringing in my ears and decided to abandon the conversation about our newly designed for-purpose approach. As we dove in deeper and deeper into the spiritual side of philanthropy, I could sense that we didn't need to rely on business lingo to demonstrate our like-mindedness.

As we continued trading ideas, Ray started to fire off recommendations and referrals. "I think that my counterpart who is responsible for the achievement of the education Millennium Development Goals, Her Highness Queen Sheikha Moza of Qatar, would be great for you to speak with." "There's also a young man you should meet with who's incredible with technology. I should introduce you to Jack Dorsey." "Do you know Maria Eitel at the Nike Foundation?" "What about Reid Hoffman at LinkedIn?" The list of world changers went on until our hour was up, and I left buzzing from head to toe.

But this was just the start of our relationship. About a month later, Ray agreed to join our board of directors. With that decision, he changed the trajectory of PoP permanently.

Ray's greatest value isn't his wallet; it's his ability to bring people together to collectively solve problems. When I decided to look further into new approaches to teacher training, literacy, and student scholarships, I started by emailing the board: *I need to speak with top education experts. Please send anyone you think I should meet with.*

Most responded with recommendations to connect with experts at universities, PhD candidates, and other for-purpose leaders. Ray wrote back, *I've been speaking a lot with the former Prime Minister of the UK, Gordon Brown, and his wife, Sarah, and I'd like to introduce you.* After my first two hours of chatting with Sarah, I knew I'd found a global leader in the education space whom I truly trusted and admired. (She would later become an honoree at our next gala.)

Ray has provided introductions to many others who have changed the trajectory of PoP, and our one-on-one conversations have always illuminated new ways to approach the issues of global education. His influence has been massive. He once advised me, "Think about how the world will change in the next ten years, and how you and your resources and networks will change within it. Use that as a compass to determine how you can affect as many people as possible." Those words have been my true north ever since.

Tehillah and Ray both taught me in different ways how transformative a single individual can be in your life. Certain people help you see a future that you could never have envisioned without their influence. They make you a better version of yourself. As the African proverb states, "If you want to go fast, go alone. If you want to go far, go together." It's the presence of others who are smarter, kinder, wiser, and different from you that enables you to evolve. Those are the people to surround yourself with at all times.

VULNERABILITY IS VITAL

In my first three years of running Pencils of Promise, an organization that desperately needed cash to grow, I did not directly ask anyone to donate a specific amount of money. Not one person.

I hated asking people for money. "I'm an entrepreneur, not a fundraiser," I repeated to anyone who would listen. I simply refused to ask.

I'd worked since I was twelve years old and always found ways to independently make and save money for the life I sought to create. So now, relying on others just didn't feel right. Asking people for favors made me feel beneath them. I didn't want to ask for money unless I could reciprocate. Although I knew plenty of people who were in a position to give a generous gift—and who didn't need anything in return—I couldn't get over asking someone I knew to open his or her wallet and write a check. I despised the idea.

But here's the truth: I was scared. Scared to face rejection.

Scared to hear no. Scared to be seen as someone who was asking for a handout. I was afraid of that moment of relinquishing control, of allowing someone to judge me. I was afraid of admitting that I couldn't do it alone. And so I didn't.

At first I thought of different ways to raise money that would spare me from personal discomfort. Selling tickets or tables to our masquerade party or annual gala was transactional. I also relied on our website to solicit donations without initiating any awkward conversations, and our industry-leading social media presence attracted corporate sponsors that offered contributions in return for marketing partnerships. These created streams of revenue for the organization that few nonprofits were able to develop, and it differentiated PoP in a crowded space, allowing us to make the case that we earned our money rather than asking for it.

The problem is, fundraising—asking individual donors, or heads of foundations, to give—is a pivotal part of leading a nonprofit organization. Building an engaged, dedicated donor base is essential to long-term success, and most major donors prefer to be asked for their support directly. Yet, I avoided it completely. With so many other essential pieces to focus on, why prioritize monetary matters when I could instead be doing what I loved—traveling around the world to work with communities that needed new schools, refining our beautiful website, and developing an incredible team that could extend our reach.

Something clicked for me when our CFO, Tom, became a father. I met his newborn son, Michael, looked into his big eyes, and realized the massive sacrifices our staff was making. Tom, and all of the people at PoP, had supported me and my dream at first, but it was now their dream too. They took lower salaries, worked insane hours, and passed up more lucrative job opportunities to create the organization we all envisioned. Now these people had children of their own, and this was no longer just my personal pursuit. I was responsible for the financial well-being of my staff, and the educational opportunities of the children we supported in countries where we worked.

I'd given up most of my social life and sleep to PoP—but I realized I'd been pouring the lion's share of my energy into the wrong things. The tasks I ignored were the ones I feared. How many times do you have thirty things to do and you focus on the twenty-five that matter least? How many times do you check your email and deal with what's easy, but not necessarily what's important? These small wins are easy to achieve, but they won't move the needle. In the end, the big wins, the most daunting tasks, are the ones that matter.

One of the most important parts of being a leader is to look in the mirror and tell the truth about what you are seeing. Even if—especially if—it's not good. And the only way to let others in is by speaking out. I decided it was time to ask for help.

At our next board meeting, after presenting my usual materials, I asked for time to share some honest thoughts. We were sitting at a conference table on the twenty-fifth floor of a Manhattan skyscraper with floor-to-ceiling windows overlooking Times Square, and instead of presenting my strongest and most impressive front, as I always tried to do at these meetings, I was going to reveal my weakness. Surrounding me were ten of the smartest, most capable people I knew. Each had achieved tremendous success in business and philanthropy, and I had to tell them about my biggest failure. I wasn't even nervous; I was resolved—that's how badly I needed help.

"I need to learn to ask people for money. This is my biggest weakness. I need to get over it." In admitting my flaw, I showed them that I was vulnerable, but that was okay. I established trust.

These were industry leaders with years of professional experience, who were each taking a gamble on me as a leader, and before that moment I'd always tried to seem invincible to the board. If they had a question, I had an answer. But in acknowledging where I needed help, I deepened my relationship with them and, ultimately, amplified their commitment to my growth as a leader and an individual.

Two of my nonprofit friends and mentors, Charles Best, the founder of DonorsChoose.org, and Scott Harrison, the founder of charity: water, recommended I participate in Exponential Fundraising, a program through the Hauser Center for Nonprofit Organizations at Harvard, taught by fundraising guru Jennifer McCrea and philanthropist Jeffrey Walker. Leaders of many sterling nonprofits had been through the program. I received a partial scholarship and the seminars were informative, but the greatest revelations came from trading war stories with Sydney, the founder of Educators 4 Excellence, and Reid, the founder of Equal Opportunity Schools. One night, after a full day of courses, we stayed up until 2:00 a.m. in the common room of our Harvard Business School dorm, both of them recounting their experiences asking wealthy philanthropists for major donations. Reid asked for $500,000 but got $250,000. Sydney asked for $50,000 and got the full amount, but now wished she'd asked for $100,000. The stories went on and on, while I sat there in silence.

"I've never asked a single person to write a specific check," I admitted.

"Never?" said Sydney.

"Never."

They couldn't believe it. Here I was with an organization that had achieved fantastic growth and broken ground on more than fifty schools, and I had yet to do the most basic task for the founder of a nonprofit. I thought, *What's wrong with me?* In asking that question I immediately realized the root of the problem.

It wasn't just about fear. It was about ego. I was putting myself at the center of the equation. I was so personally attached to PoP that I felt as though I were asking for myself. I didn't recognize that the *ask* wasn't for me. I was just an ambassador for the organization and for the children we served.

With four offices around the world, thousands of students in our schools, and millions of educational hours being delivered, this was about something bigger. It was about our first students Nith and Nuth, four-year-old girls, who now had a preschool to attend. It was about the second-graders in Guatemala who were learning to read and write for the first time in a Pencils of Promise school. The money I asked for wasn't for me; it was for them. It was to change their lives, not mine. As soon as I shifted my focus to the children and our staff, I suddenly became excited to make an ask. It no longer felt like a burden. It suddenly became an honor.

Soon I had my first opportunity. I had met Paul Foster, a New York–based investor, six months earlier at our gala. He was a friend of our event producer and bought a table to attend the event. During the night I invited supporters to join me on a trip to Laos for contributing at a certain level. Twenty hands shot up, thousands of dollars were raised, but when I flew to Laos several months later only one family had made it their top priority to fly halfway around the world to meet me on the ground. The Fosters.

As soon as I landed, Lanoy picked me up with her Shark Book in hand and we drove straight to Lemongrass Restaurant in Luang Prabang to meet Paul and his family. In the days ahead we visited Pha Theung to see the first school, swam in the river with the children, and found ourselves sleeping in a shared bamboo hut in the remote village of Phayong. Paul and I bonded that week, and he told me his story of working as a head trader at a well-known investment bank, becoming president of a leading hedge fund that he grew to $20 billion in assets, and then leaving it all to retire and focus on raising his kids at the age of forty-five.

When we returned to the states, Paul and his family visited the PoP office. The Laos trip had been an awakening experience for the entire family. Paul pulled me aside and told me that he wanted to be more involved. Here was my opportunity. I decided I would ask Paul to be the first to join our advisory board—a commitment of three years and $250,000 per year. It was a huge ask, but I figured I might as well go big the first time around and see what happened.

I asked Paul if we could meet up the next month in New York City, and he suggested a prestigious private club in midtown.

"You'll have to wear a jacket and tie," he said.

I hated dressing in business attire, so I wore my black jeans to the meeting. Paul, whom I had only seen wearing shorts while in Laos, met me by the club's sprawling carpeted staircase. I looked up. He was in a power suit: pinstripes with a tailored shirt and sharp tie. I looked down. My faded jeans had holes on the cuffs. I felt like an idiot.

He greeted me kindly and led me to the dining room. He passed me the lunch menu and recommended several of the entrées. I had just started my first ever juice fast. I ordered a grapefruit juice with embarrassment.

"Really," quipped Paul, eating a delicious-looking salad with salmon. "A juice fast? I've heard about these things. How is it going?"

"Honestly, I feel good. I'm on day four, but I haven't felt hungry until this very moment."

He laughed, and finally the ice was broken. Paul opened up

to me about how meaningful the trip to Laos was for him and his family. Toward the end of the meal, he spoke about how much he wanted to help. "Most people would not leave Bain to do this, and I want to know how I can be supportive," he said.

Here was my chance. "Paul, your words mean so much to me. Truthfully, I am trying to put together an advisory board for the organization made up of people who are deeply invested in our work. It would mean the world to me if you were the first to commit. This would entail you and I speaking regularly so I could gain your mentorship and advice. I would also love for you to introduce me to anyone else who you think would be a good fit, and I would like you to consider making a three-year commitment"—I wanted to say, "of $250,000 per year," but chickened out and instead said, "of six figures per year to Pencils of Promise." My face was still, but my chest was pounding.

Paul paused. "Six figures per year is a big commitment. Keep in mind I'm currently retired, so I don't have an active income."

It wasn't a no. I still had time to maneuver.

"Would you consider $100,000 per year?" I asked.

"Let me talk to my wife and get back to you," he said. "I love what you're doing so I really want to be helpful. Let's take off, though, since I have to get home, but I'm really glad we did this and let me know how the juice fast goes."

I left feeling exhausted and relieved. I'd made the ask, although it didn't go as smoothly as I'd hoped. Whether successful or not, I was taking steps forward on behalf of the organization. I sent Paul a nice thank-you email, along with some materials to help consider the request.

Two weeks later I still hadn't heard back. I was getting worried when I finally got an email from him: "Can you give me a call?"

I called him right away. We made small talk for a few minutes, but we both knew the purpose of the conversation. I was pacing back and forth in my office as he said, "Adam, this was a big family decision. My wife and I discussed this at length. It was not something we took lightly." Then—just as I was mentally prepared for him to tell me that they weren't comfortable with the financial commitment—he told me what I was hoping to hear. "We believe in you and we want to support you. We are going to do $100,000 per year for the next three years."

This was amazing news. I pumped my fist in the air.

"Here's the thing, though, how are you with feedback?"

"Good, great, please tell me," I said, bracing myself for whatever was next.

"First, Adam, if you are asking people for large sums of money, you need to dress the part. You can't wear jeans to a meeting at a private members club. You have to get a nice suit.

"Second, is follow-up. The difference between good leaders and great leaders is in the details. At the end of our meeting I asked you to tell me about how the juice fast went. You told me you'd let me know, but you didn't. If you make a commitment to inform me about how your juice fast goes, you have to let me know how the juice fast goes. You need to find a deliberate system so that you are relentless with your follow-up. Nothing should slip through the cracks. This is where I excelled, and it's going to become integral to your ultimate success."

Paul has since introduced me to countless stellar people, many of whom have become significant funders of our work. Immediately after each meeting, I now send out a follow-up email detailing the commitments made by both sides so there's mutual alignment. Paul then calls them to ask what they think, gains critical feedback, and calls me to relay exactly what was strong and weak about my performance in the meeting. I now have someone who is brutally honest with me on a daily basis and coaches me through my greatest areas of personal growth.

We all spend so much time putting up walls so that others can't see our vulnerabilities, but those same walls often enclose us within our own insecurities. By showing my true hand to my board of directors, they helped me turn a weakness that I was avoiding into a newfound strength. We all know which tasks are the most important in any given day, yet we still choose to do them last. Choose to do those things first.

When I initially asked Paul to invest I was hoping to get over my fear of asking for money to support our organization. His generosity helped in that area, but I ultimately gained so much more. I got over parts of myself that were holding us back, and I learned that the hardest climbs are the ones that yield the most reward.

LISTEN TO YOUR ECHOES

Since PoP's inception, the main way that we'd communicated with our supporters was through digital content, and as we grew, we desperately needed someone to run our social media presence. Brad and I had been doing it for years, but it eventually became a part-time job in itself, requiring someone to monitor our feed round the clock. Your most valuable commodity is your time, and we needed to spend ours meeting with our biggest donors face-to-face.

One afternoon, in walked a twenty-two-year-old guy with a full mouth of braces applying for an assistant position. Dressed in a stylish black shirt and red, skinny tie, Carlo was so nervous during his first interview that his mouth ran dry and he left to get a glass of water so he could continue speaking. But despite the nerves we saw in the meeting, his personal Twitter feed reflected a confident, engaging voice that made us want to bring him on board. As he walked toward the elevator after his final-round interview, I used my favorite tactic to get someone to commit to working for us. I asked him not to send me a traditional follow-up email that night, but to take a few days and send me a marathon letter from the heart about whether he wanted the role. If he was unsure, in writing that letter he'd convince himself of just how much he wanted it. That weekend, I got his note:

> *I do not think I can be as focused and dedicated to the cause as I would like to be working only two days a week, so I am willing to decline the internship offer I received at Bad Boy Worldwide, a position I previously believed I always wanted, if offered this position at Pencils of Promise, for the cause, staff, and work environment of your company have already captured my heart. I am willing to come in 4 days a week, but I would like to spend Friday and Saturday working part-time so I will not have to be financially dependent on my parents for the next year if offered the position. . . .*

Two weeks later, Carlo started as an administrative assistant at PoP. He eventually taught himself to run all of our social media accounts and to write code, and he became our lead designer too. By having someone with design skills leading our messaging, the brand became more beautiful and engaging. When he doubled our digital following within months, it became apparent that I had a lot to learn from him about building a community online as well.

The more he progressed, the more Carlo took off my plate. As his confidence grew, he not only freed me up to start putting Paul Foster's lessons to work by securing new major donors, but he also became a leader among our young staff. He was more than the eyes and ears of the organization, he established himself as the glue that held it together too.

At the time, it was clear that everyone expected us to keep growing. Expectations are the daunting shadows that trail behind accomplishments; no matter how high one goes, the other follows on its footsteps. We couldn't rest on our previous successes, so we had to keep identifying ways to inspire others. I was out on the road pursuing potential donors one afternoon when Carlo wrote to me about the girl who would inspire us to finally launch our next big campaign:

AB, you're not going to believe the tweet I just saw. Check out our Twitter feed.

The post had been written by a seventeen-year-old girl in California named Kennedy Donnelly, and at first glance I thought it was a hoax: *Biking across America to raise money for @Pencilsofpromise, follow my blog www.pedalingforpencils.blogspot.com.*

Was she serious? I sent her a quick message to make sure her parents knew of the plan. They were on board. She had discovered PoP online and become so passionate about our mission that she had committed to ride thirty-eight hundred miles across the entire United States to raise $10,000 to build a new classroom. I was floored.

She explained that when she had the original idea, others told her that it was crazy. They told her it would be impossible. But the more they doubted her, the more it motivated her. In her words: "At first I was playing around with the idea, but the more that people told me that I couldn't do it, the more committed I became."

We'd noticed a lot of people launching fundraisers on our website that required them to take on personal challenges with seemingly insurmountable odds. Some raised as little as $25, others raised in excess of $50,000. The common thread seemed to be their belief in the value of education, and a desire to reach for an aspirational goal.

We needed a way to capture this and decided to build something around this idea to unify these people. We launched a campaign called the Impossible Ones, just as I'd discussed with the students on Semester at Sea, which celebrated those who took on new challenges in support of our mission. We asked supporters to either donate toward these efforts or to launch a fundraiser of their own to help us reach the "impossible goal" of our hundredth school.

Kennedy's pursuit embodied the same spirit through which PoP had been forged and became one of the stories Carlo featured on the campaign website. Her story of hope galvanized thousands of others to sign up and take on their own challenge too. After Kennedy rode for fifty-five days across the country, we held a huge welcome party for her at our brand-new Manhattan office, which Larry's team had built out, just as he had promised.

My brother Scott was in town, after having joined me on a trip to Guatemala where we opened a school dedicated in his honor. He had asked for donations rather than gifts for his thirtieth birthday and had raised more than $30,000 as a result. Our trip to Guatemala not only brought us closer together as siblings, but it brought him closer to the work he'd been supporting for years. Nick Onken joined us on a day's notice to shoot photos of our newest schools, and by the time we left, Scott insisted, "I'm going to cover my entire office with the photos from this trip. I want every person I meet with to ask me about Pencils of Promise."

When he met Kennedy, he asked to hear her story too. She told him of her long, grueling days riding under the hot sun and her restless nights sleeping in public parks. He asked how much she'd hoped to raise. She proudly said, "Ten thousand dollars, and I just reached it this week."

"Are you sure? I heard you actually raised twenty thousand dollars," he said with a smile.

"I wish! It's taken me months to raise ten thousand dollars."

"Well, I've got good news for you. I'm going to donate another ten thousand dollars to your campaign. You just raised twenty thousand dollars."

Her jaw dropped. Her eyes started to well up, and her hands began to shake. She couldn't believe it. After regaining her composure, she jokingly blurted out, "I should have just started here!" As everyone cracked up, she added, "But seriously, your support of PoP means the world to me."

"I could say the same to you," Scott replied, smiling ear to ear.

One of the other stories we featured as part of the Impossible Ones was that of Joel Runyon, a blogger whose website, ImpossibleHQ, helped people take on the impossible. He committed to running his first ultramarathon to build a new school, and in response his subscribers rallied over several months to raise $25,000 on his behalf. After visiting his school to meet the kids in person, he posted before and after pictures on his blog and wrote, *It would be almost impossible to pull off something like this on my own, but PoP's mission to create opportunities with sustainable models and ongoing community programs is one of the things that I love about them. They're not just there to build a school and leave; they're there to build a school to help change the community.* As I read that, I started to realize those words were no longer mine. They now belonged to Joel and Kennedy and Scott—and with that, they were reverberating forward with more force than I'd ever imagined possible.

Countless other Impossible Ones were extending our message. Sophia Bush aimed to raise $30,000 for her thirtieth birthday, just as Scott had done the year before, and her fans ended up more than doubling her goal by contributing nearly $70,000. When asked why she supported us, she responded, "Because I want young girls to know that the sexiest part of their body is their brain, and education is the way forward for them. PoP gives me that opportunity."

Thousands of individuals and groups have created fundraisers to support PoP since our start. One family raised $250 by selling $1 pencils; a company raised $5,000 by donating the proceeds of their annual holiday party; a thirteen-year-old girl raised $22,000 by asking for donations instead of bat mitzvah gifts. I got into the habit of beginning my day searching for articles about people who had made PoP a focal part of their lives. As I watched our school-count rise and read about why it meant so much to these people, it dawned on me that meeting our growing expectations would not be dependent on my voice alone carrying the message forward.

If an idea grows, it expands far beyond the confines of any one person's control. By limiting it to a single story told by a single voice, we strip it of its true potential. The role of the founder should eventually be to listen to the echoes of his or her initial words, and then encourage and amplify the most genuine among those you hear. The more I embraced this as my true role, the more I became inspired by the journeys of the individuals, families, and companies in our PoP community.

Our success was now in the hands of any person who made the choice that it was more important to educate a child than to receive birthday gifts that year. Our growth would be dictated by how many people decided that Back to School campaigns should be used to ensure that more children actually returned to school the following year. The number of lives we impacted would not be determined by my efforts alone, or even PoP's efforts, but by the efforts of every person who decided that 57 million children without access to education wasn't just a concern, it was a crisis that urgently needed to be solved.

*   *   *

In an effort to understand how we could amplify our impact, I decided to sit down with the most knowledgeable people I could find in the global education space. Week after week we opened a new school, steadily progressing toward our hundredth. Our work demonstrated with hard data that 85 percent of teachers in communities with PoP schools saw gains in literacy and 88 percent saw improvements in mathematics. Students in PoP schools scored three times higher on tests than students in non-PoP neighboring community schools. But was that enough? Should we continue to just engage communities through school building, or did we need to expand our core programs further? I figured that because I'd only worked in the space for several years, someone else had to have the silver bullet to solving the global education crisis. If I could just find out that one thing that would most improve the lives of children in poverty, perhaps PoP could galvanize others to rally around that single solution. Yet in conversation after conversation, I heard differing opinions.

What I have ultimately come to realize is that education is complex. You can't inject someone with education the way you can with a vaccine. You can't force it upon people. They have to reach out and work for it themselves. Such a fragmented issue requires a fragmented set of solutions.

Every child needs several key things to attain a quality education. Most important among these are a safe place to learn, a support system of well-trained teachers and invested parents, and the ability to progress from year to year as the cost of learning increases. We wanted to dedicate ourselves to making these things realities for communities around the world.

The opinion that ultimately shaped our future course of action, though, was not my own, but that of our staff in the field. My voice may have set our initial vision, but they experienced the impact of our work every single day, and their voices rose with candor and confidence when deciding what our future programs should entail. Based on their recommendations, we decided that it was important to go beyond just building schools and move into teacher training and student scholarships as well.

As we developed these programs, I constantly asked myself, would we one day be able to reach the level of impact that we envisioned? But the future of the organization was no longer mine to determine. It belonged to our staff and supporters. It was the progression of people like Carlo that would guide the next great PoP campaign. It was the inspiring story of someone like Kennedy that would draw in our next supporter. And it was no longer just my birthday that would help us raise funds, but the birthdays of thousands of people like Sophia and Scott that would be used to provide the gift of education to others.

IF YOUR DREAMS DON'T SCARE YOU, THEY'RE NOT BIG ENOUGH

PoP was on the verge of completing its hundredth school by early 2013. When we realized the milestone school would be opened in Ghana, I made plans to attend the ceremony. I hadn't been there in fifteen months, and I was too excited to sleep on the overnight Delta flight from JFK to Accra. When I deplaned, Freeman, our country director, gave me a warm embrace at baggage claim.

"Welcome, Adam!" he shouted. "We have a busy week ahead, my friend."

As soon as we stepped outside, I was bathed in heat, a stark contrast to New York City's January freeze. Women balancing baskets of soda and candy on their heads were selling local goods to buses at traffic lights. Music played loudly from passing cars as young boys dangled their arms out the windows, ready to wave at giggling girls—proving that teenagers are teenagers in every country.

When we arrived at my small hotel in Accra, Freeman told me to get some sleep because the next few days would be long and exhausting. We had many villages to visit, communities to evaluate, and conversations with local authorities ahead.

In an effort to share our work on the ground, I decided to post a one-minute video montage of the previous twenty-four hours on YouTube each night. Despite Freeman's advice, I stayed up until 3:00 a.m. to work on the first video message. Alone in my room, sitting on a hard bed like the ones that I had grown accustomed to from my backpacking days, I heard quiet conversations coming from the hallway. A group of American study-abroad students were discussing their plans for the upcoming semester in Accra. They talked about their friends' latest updates on Facebook, comedians they followed on Twitter, and Skyping with their parents. They had no idea what the next few months would hold, but they wanted to experience everything. They wanted to live deeply and fully. They sounded like Impossible Ones.

Back at home, in the PoP office, staffers had a mix of elation and reflection as we approached the opening of the hundredth school—a goal that we had set nearly two years before. Every person at PoP felt tremendous pride in the scope of our impact over four short years. We had exceeded every single expectation others put before us—and outshot our own ambitions as well. But if reaching peak performance is difficult, maintaining it is nearly impossible. I needed to determine how to sustain our momentum. What audacious new goals could I set to motivate our staff and supporters that were still attainable?

It had taken just over four years to break ground on the first hundred schools. But as all of those business courses and consulting projects taught me, organizational growth is rarely linear. Acceleration rates, when mapped out, usually produce S or J curves because growth can become exponential. I couldn't look at the pace of the past to determine our future. We had to intensify our scale and more deeply invest into our existing communities to produce true centers of excellence.

I knew I needed help in this next phase, so I called in the experts. The Bridgespan Group, a nonprofit adviser founded by Bain partners, selected us to participate in a special program designed to take stellar organizations to the next level. Something about going back to Bain on my own terms at this point in the journey was poetic. It reminded me of the many steps that had led here and how each of them—even though I didn't always realize it at the time—was meaningful and essential.

Over several months of strategic sessions with Bridgespan, we developed a new set of goals that were big, but that we could stand firmly behind. We decided to focus on expanding our traditional school builds and developing our new teacher-training and student-scholarships programs. We recognized that children don't just need safe structures in which to learn, but also qualified teachers and supportive elements, including uniforms, textbooks, and transportation. We set new goals to reach our five hundredth school, train a thousand teachers, and provide ten thousand student scholarships by the end of 2015. To reach these benchmarks we would need to break ground on a hundred new schools in 2013 alone. What had taken us four years to accomplish previously, we hoped to replicate in just one year.

I announced this new goal to our team a week before I left for Ghana, and while part of my trip to the field would be celebratory, much of it would be used strategically to launch our next phase. After our initial meeting with a peer organization in Accra, we spent the next three days bouncing around dirt paths and visiting villages that had requested new schools in the Volta Region, where PoP Ghana was headquartered.

The poverty was rampant. Families lived in mud huts, corrugated-tin shacks, or basic cement homes. Electricity and running water were luxuries. Children in tattered clothes milled about, eyeing us curiously. In one community we witnessed hundreds of children learning under large mango trees. They had no formal classrooms, only a series of desks grouped together in front of chalkboards nailed to tree trunks. When one teacher told me that he taught the older children ICT (information and communications technology), I asked how that was possible. He explained that they had never seen a computer. Instead, he drew a keyboard with chalk and they practiced typing letters on the board. "What happens if there is too much heat, dust, or rain outside?" I asked. He looked at me blankly and said, "Then we have no school that week."

As we walked away, Freeman tapped me on the shoulder. "We break ground on a new school here in four months' time. At the start of the next school year, the children will have their first true classrooms. It will be a very happy day."

We held meetings with village chiefs, elders, principals, teachers, and parents, and every community was committed to bettering their children's education. But our evaluation process required several meetings before a project could move forward, and we needed to gather more information on a few of the places we had visited to determine the best-suited communities in which to begin.

To gain more insight we visited Volta Region's education ministry. Freeman had arranged for me to meet with the director of the education ministry, his key officials, and our direct contact there, a young, superstar employee aptly named Bright Dey. After a few minutes of driving toward Ho, our beat-up SUV stopped along the side of the road and the door swung open.

"You are most welcome to Ghana," Bright said, hopping into our truck. "We are quite pleased to have you join us, Mr. Adam. Yes, I have heard many wonderful things about your story, with the pencils. It is agreeable to us that we should make a world that educates every child, in particular the children in poverty. But we must do this together. Yes, together."

Yes, together, I repeated in my head as we drove on. Upon our arrival at the education ministry, Bright walked us into the small, dimly lit waiting area, before inviting us to join a presentation about the Volta Region's educational system. After a series of formal introductions, Bright presented a lengthy PowerPoint that demonstrated the area's greatest needs using graphs, charts, diagrams, and statistics. Primary school infrastructure, teacher training, and secondary matriculation were highlighted. This region and the team were clearly a perfect fit for our expansion plans in those areas. The director then discussed his desire to work with partner NGOs like Pencils of Promise. The meeting ended with warm handshakes all around, and commitments to visit each other again. I secretly wished that all of my meetings were like this one. Too often I was not a part of these local meetings anymore since most of my responsibilities were back in New York City.

At a company's inception, the founder is usually the one creating the product or delivering the service. The guy who creates a massive pizza chain probably started by making and hand-delivering the pizza himself. The woman who oversees a major fashion line most likely began by drawing sketches, cutting cloth, and selling the first samples out of her apartment.

The bittersweet reality of business is that as things grow, founders find themselves more and more removed from the creation of their product. Their greatest value lies elsewhere, often as a representative of the brand. In the first few years of PoP, I was the only one on the ground, spending months of my year in the field working with village chiefs, teachers, and education ministries. As we expanded, that became the responsibility of our local staff on the ground.

I knew this would happen. In fact I was proud that local PoP staff were now taking on more responsibility. Few things inspired me more than witnessing a staff member who'd grown up in a bamboo hut with no running water or electricity now organizing digital photos into PowerPoint presentations while uploading Excel documents to teams across the world via Dropbox. But I still missed those moments in the field, sharing stories and laughter across cultures. And deep down I was somewhat worried about whether others would feel as strongly about our work as I did.

The next morning, when we arrived in the hilltop village of Goviefe Todzi, chairs and tents were arranged around the school grounds to protect the elderly villagers from the blistering heat. Behind me sat George from Ashesi University, a Ghanaian student I'd met when I returned to lecture on SAS, and a bus full of his Ghanaian classmates who created the Ashesi University PoP chapter. They had organized concerts and sold shirts to help fund this school. I couldn't help but feel inspired by their commitment.

The ceremony kicked off with the students marching into the square, singing traditional songs and dancing to the beat of djembe drums. Two grandmothers rose from their seats to dance in the square as well, reminding all in attendance that this was a family affair—and that brittle bones could still boogie. When the music ended, the village deputy announced each of the distinguished guests. A district official spoke of her own journey, emphasizing the importance of her studies, and concluded with one of my favorite quotes: "If you think education is expensive, try ignorance."

Following the speeches, I helped the children carry their wooden benches into the school to set up their classroom. Just then local hip-hop music blared through the loudspeakers. I couldn't see where it was coming from, but it sounded like it was emanating from the other side of the school.

I sat down with the village leaders for a meal of delicious red-red, a popular Ghanaian dish of bean stew with fried plantains. Men and women shared jokes while sipping on bottled Coca-Cola and Fanta, but as much as I tried to focus on the conversations in front of me, my mind kept drifting toward the blasting music from the schoolyard. My favorite part of school openings in our other countries had always been the dancing. "I'll be right back," I said quietly, and slipped away from the table.

When I rounded the corner, I saw something I almost couldn't believe. More than a hundred kids, ages five to fifteen, were furiously dancing in the schoolyard, sweating through their bright orange uniforms, and sending dust from the ground into the air. They saw me and grabbed my hands, pulling me into the middle of their circle, cheering with delight. No adults were in sight, and without the glaring eyes of judgment around us, for the next twenty minutes I danced harder than I ever had in my life. A student would teach me a move that I'd replicate to the laughter of the kids, and then I would teach him one in return. The funky chicken, the tootsie roll, the disco fever—all of the moves I'd perfected in my childhood bedroom played well in Ghana. I moved and a schoolyard of kids would mimic my move. The noon heat beat down on us, sweating profusely and laughing uncontrollably. As the dust filled in the air around us, we celebrated to a single rhythm.

Dancing with these kids, I looked around and acknowledged that what you see around you is proof of what exists within you. There is a primal energy that spurs us to move, to shake, to transform. And once ignited, it is a feeling that takes on a life of its own. I remembered how special that first school opening was to me, the one dedicated to Ma, and realized that every one of the other ninety-nine felt that special to someone else. It meant that much to the donor who bought the cement, the mother and the father who laid the bricks, and the child who would now learn to read her first word from her first book.

I thought of Ma, and Joel Puac, and Lanoy, standing proudly with her Shark Book. But I was ready to move on from past stories, from past schools, from past achievements. I now saw it all as a continuum. I thought of the thousands of students who were in PoP schools at that very moment. I pictured our next hundred schools and the hundred schools after that, and the impact they would have around the world.

Ellen Johnson Sirleaf, the first female elected head of state in Africa, said, "If your dreams do not scare you, they are not big enough." We had reached a once unattainable goal, but now it was time to stretch our work further. True motivation is not found within reaching a goal, but rather getting to a place where you can confidently and audaciously move the finish line far off into the distance once again. It's in the space between the known and the unknown, where you can craft a vision for the future that you hope to create and then chase it with relentless fervor. Though I didn't know exactly how we'd navigate every turn ahead, I knew that we already had the roadmap to reach our greatest aspirations.

By giving people of all ages and backgrounds an organization through which they could leave their own mark, individuals that I didn't yet know would bring each new school to life, making our story their story too. Through Pencils of Promise they would change the lives of others in the same way that Chelsea Canada and Rich Lent and Kennedy Donnelly had. They would become the next Brad Haugen or Hope Taitz or Ray Chambers of the Pencils of Promise narrative. They would become the gatekeepers of that infectious energy that had propelled the organization forward from the start.

Because as long as somewhere in the world a child still stands with an outstretched hand asking for nothing more than a pencil, our mission will continue on.

EPILOGUE TO THE PAPERBACK
Make your life a story worth telling

As of the date of the paperback publication of this book, Pencils of Promise has broken ground on more than 250 schools, delivered over 25 million educational hours, and is opening a new school every ninety hours. But we don't just build four walls and move on; we are committed to the long-term support and sustainability of every project we undertake. Our comprehensive approach to educational attainment has led to recognition by the World Economic Forum and the Clinton Global Initiative, and most recently, to being awarded Education Organization of the Year at a showcase held at the United Nations. Going forward we are launching a series of innovations that will test new technologies and teaching methods we believe will be truly game-changing.

Please consider supporting our work by providing a scholarship, training a teacher, or building the next Pencils of Promise school at www.PencilsofPromise.org. It costs only $25 to educate a child, $500 to train a teacher, and $25,000 to build a school. More than thirty thousand people have created unique fundraisers on our website to educate children. Perhaps your upcoming birthday will be next.

Lanoy is now the country director of PoP Laos, where she leads more than thirty local staff members. After nearly four years in Laos, Leslie moved to New York City, where she now leads all PoP International Programs globally. Brad was elected chairman of our board of directors, and Nick Onken continues to travel to each country where we work to shoot photography for the organization. It's been years since Joel Puac took me into his home, but I went back to find him and tell him about everything that had occurred because of his initial hospitality. When I found him in the mountains and told him about what Pencils of Promise had become, he disappeared into his home momentarily. When he emerged from his bedroom, he was smiling ear to ear, holding in his hand that very same tape recorder I'd spoken into years earlier. The cassettes we recorded had worn down, but he explained that his children now spoke solid English.

Pencils of Promise currently employs more than seventy staff members in our countries of impact, over 90 percent of whom are locals. They work to keep the opportunity to learn alive for children like Nith and Nuth, who are now star fourth-graders. A commitment that began with a promise to those three young girls has now expanded into an organization that has directly educated more than thirty-five thousand children. This is no longer my story. This is now their story too.

When I think back to how this all began, one thing is incredibly clear: I was hopelessly idealistic from the start. I use the word *hope-*

lessly purposely, as my belief in PoP has always been devoid of hope. I never thought, *I hope this works out.* I knew it would. From the moment that first bolt of electric energy hit me at the New York Philharmonic, I never once questioned whether the organization would succeed. That's because it went beyond passion and felt like purpose. Purpose is found when you stop thinking about how you exist in the world and start trying to figure out why you are here. Once you solve that question, everything else will fall into place.

I was only twenty-four when I made that first $25 bank deposit. But while many perceive youth as a weakness, it's actually an incredible strength. The single most powerful element of youth is that you don't have the life experiences to know what can't be done. While others highlight the value of wisdom, wisdom also remembers that achieving certain things was hard, if not impossible. Young people don't carry that burden. They're too naive to realize what can't be accomplished, and in that fact lies their willingness to try.

Martin Luther King Jr. was just twenty-six when he led the Montgomery Bus Boycott. Steve Jobs created Apple when he was twenty-one, Bill Gates founded Microsoft at twenty, and Mark Zuckerberg started Facebook when he was only nineteen. The most prominent voice in global education is seventeen-year-old Malala Yousafzai, who against all odds survived being shot in the head while on her way to school, and who still stands every day as a powerful voice for change in defiance of Taliban oppression. For any young person reading this book, my message is clear. Never let anyone tell you that your dream is impossible. No matter how big or small, you can make it real.

For anyone going through a restless period in life, looking to make a change but not sure how, start with an ambitious but attainable goal. I set out to build just one school. Only after I realized that it was possible and how much of a difference it made in the life of others did I focus on enabling anyone else to have that same experience too. The key is to think big and then take small, incremental steps forward day by day.

Start by changing the subjects of your daily conversation from the life you are living to the life you aspire to create. By speaking the language of the person you seek to become, you will soon find yourself immersed in the conversations that make you most come alive. You'll sense the energy you emit attracting similar energy from others. Your conversations will lead to opportunities, which will become actions, which will become footprints for good.

But you can't keep saying, "I'll get started tomorrow." The world has far too many problems, and you are way too smart and capable not to help tackle them. Your time is now.

Since the hardcover edition of this book was released, I have been so moved by the emails that I've received from readers. Many of these notes have been deeply personal, and yet they consistently prove that although sadness takes many forms, all of them are conquerable. These letters demonstrate that the human spirit is far more inventive, resilient, and interconnected than I could have possibly imagined. You can find my contact information on the pages ahead, and I truly hope that you will send me a personal note upon your completion of this book as well.

I used to send out lengthy email updates to my family and friends while backpacking, and people consistently said, "You should publish something." I appreciated their responses, but I didn't think the travel tales of a backpacker warranted a full book unless an impactful organization was born out of the things I learned on the road. But those comments got me thinking. As humans, we are natural storytellers. We weave narrative into nearly every relationship we build and value. I realized that I needed to live a life that reflected the themes of the stories I wanted to one day tell, and when I veered off that path later on, it was time to make a change. Regardless of age or status, if you're not satisfied with the path you're on, it's time to rewrite your future. Your life should be a story you are excited to tell.

On a beautiful spring day just two months after the hardcover release of this book, Tehillah and I were married in front of our closest family and friends. A new chapter will begin in my life in the years ahead, one that includes building not just schools but a family too. I'll be sure to teach my children the value of my mother's favorite word, *integrity*, the essence of Dad's Rules, and each of the mantras that title the chapters of this book. I'll tell them that the most direct route to happiness is through creating joy for someone else, and that change doesn't happen through hard work alone. It requires strength of imagination. It relies on that ability we each possess to suspend belief in the restraints of today to enable the possibilities of tomorrow. Most of all, I'll remind them each morning that we make a choice to bring positivity or negativity into the world, and that within every single person there lies an extraordinary story waiting to unfold.

ACKNOWLEDGMENTS

Although this book focuses heavily on the story of one of my grandmothers, Eva, I'd like to start by acknowledging my grandmother Dorothy. She was left to raise three children alone when my mother's dad died, and has been my biggest supporter as a writer throughout my entire life. Thank you for your words of encouragement, your daily heroism, and your continued love, Grandma. This book would never have been written if not for you. Mom and Dad, thank you for your unending support, your willingness to listen to my rants at all hours, and for being the best role models I could imagine. Liza, Scott, Sam, and Cornelio, I'm so proud of each of you. You inspire me every single day, and I hope that one day my children will be surrounded by siblings as incredible as each of you. Ma, Apu, Grandpa Sam, Grandpa Irving, and the rest of the family, if I could hug all of you right now I would hold on for hours. And to my guardian angel, Tehillah, thank you for your love, your patience, and your partnership. Now and forever.

To my writing partner, Carlye Adler, thank you for your heart, your wisdom, and your friendship. I value you more than I could ever put into words. To the dream team of Simon Green and Shannon Welch, without you two this book wouldn't have existed. You both believed that this story needed to be told, and I am so grateful to you for making that happen.

Semester at Sea was the best and most transformational experience of my life, and I would be remiss not to state how thankful I am to have had the chance to board the MV *Explorer*. Without SAS, this would have been a very different story. I'd also like to thank everyone at Brown University, Bain & Company, GHS, 5 Euclid Avenue, and the 75 Second Avenue crew for bringing so much joy into my life. I love you all and wouldn't change a single second of our time together.

There are far too many people in the Pencils of Promise family to thank, so to every person who has ever had an @pencilsof promise.org email address, attended our events, worked in the field, sat on our board, joined a local leadership council, started a chapter at their school, created a PoP fundraiser, contributed toward our work, or shared our message in any capacity, I am eternally grateful to you. You've brought so much light into the lives of so many children, and I will be forever humbled by your commitment and generosity.

Visit www.AdamBraun.com/Book
to read the bonus chapter and see photos

- Find free readers guides for each chapter
- Preview posters of your favorite mantras
- See photos and videos from the field
- Learn how to build the next PoP school
- Subscribe to learn more insider tips
- Ask any question directly to the author
- Bring the author to your event

To contact Adam directly, please email adam@ipromise.org

#PoPbook

THE
PROMISE
OF A PENCIL

How an Ordinary Person
Can Create Extraordinary Change

ADAM BRAUN

with Carlye Adler

INTRODUCTION

Adam Braun began working summers at hedge funds when he was just sixteen years old, sprinting down the path to a successful Wall Street career. But while traveling in India he met a young boy begging on the streets, who, after being asked what he wanted most in the world, answered simply, "A pencil." This small request led to a staggering series of events that took Braun backpacking through dozens of countries before eventually leaving one of the world's most prestigious jobs to found Pencils of Promise, the organization he started with just $25 that has since built more than 250 schools around the world.

The Promise of a Pencil chronicles Braun's journey to find his calling. Each chapter explains one clear step that every person can take to turn their biggest ambitions into reality, even starting with as little as $25. His story takes readers behind the scenes with business moguls and village chiefs, world-famous celebrities and hometown heroes. Driven by compelling stories and shareable insights, this is a vivid and inspiring book that will give you the tools to make your own life a story worth telling.

TOPICS & QUESTIONS
FOR DISCUSSION

1. In the opening of *The Promise of a Pencil*, Adam shares the details of his personal lineage. From his grandparents' Holocaust survival and time spent in concentration camps to his parents' decision to take in two boys from Mozambique, it's clear that his family's journey had an immense impact on him. What elements of your childhood most shaped your present worldview?

2. Adam applied to the Semester at Sea program in order to get out of his comfort zone. Why do you think this is important, and how can you practice getting out of your own comfort zone, in small or big ways?

3. Adam describes the film *Baraka* and the music of Bob Dylan as instrumental in his informal education. Which films, songs, and albums changed your life? Are there any works of literature or music that you've always wanted to absorb but haven't yet?

4. In the chapter titled "Do the small things that make others feel big," Adam discusses the role of the business cards he received as a fundraising coordinator for the Cambodian Children's Fund. Which small gifts or acts of inclusion made you feel deeply connected to a broader whole in your life? Is there anything you could do today to extend that feeling to others?

5. What do you view as the differences between a tourist and a traveler?

6. Adam began struggling at his management consultant job when his passion for Pencils of Promise grew, but he still had responsibilities to his work. Have you ever been in this dilemma, and how did you choose to balance these competing interests?

7. If you were at the groundbreaking of the first PoP school in Laos, how would you describe the experience? Why do you think it's so important that Pencils of Promise requires local communities to provide 10 to 20 percent of the cost for each school build?

8. The catalyst for the first school was to honor Adam's grandmother. How can you most powerfully celebrate or honor someone special in your life in the coming months?

9. How would you define an "impossible one"? Do you fit into that category, or does someone you know? What characteristics does this person embody that you can adopt?

10. Why is it important to create separation to build connection? How does Adam practice this, and how can you achieve this in your life?

11. What does "closing the loop" mean? How can you use the lessons that Adam learned about following up with others?

12. What inspired the term "for-purpose," and how does Adam define it? Can you think of other organizations that use this model? Why do you think so many organizations are blending profit and purpose in today's society?

13. Adam speaks about the importance of surrounding yourself with the people who will help you grow. Who are positive people in your life, and how can you foster those relationships?

14. Adam refers to the Ellen Johnson Sirleaf quote, "If your dreams don't scare you, they are not big enough." Which dreams in your current life scare you most, and are you willing to run toward them at full speed?

15. A fundamental message throughout the book is that where you start in life shouldn't dictate where you finish, and the single most impactful way to rectify this injustice is through education. How will you get involved with Pencils of Promise's goal of solving the global education crisis?

ENHANCE YOUR BOOK CLUB

1. Watch videos of Adam's latest talks or read his insightful blogs, as he shares multimedia storytelling and the latest lessons learned on www.adambraun.com/blog. Follow his musings on Twitter (www.twitter.com/adambraun) and join him on his round-the-world adventures that are always shared on Instagram (www.instagram.com/itsadambraun).

2. Bring Adam as a guest speaker to your college, conference, or company event. He travels constantly as a keynote speaker. Learn more at www.adambraun.com/speaking or email him directly at adam@ipromise.org.

3. Help build the next Pencils of Promise school, train a PoP teacher, or provide a student with a new scholarship! Get involved at www.mypopstory.org.

Ready for your next step?

Get started today:

MYPOPSTORY.ORG